over-
committed

rushaholics

the
mindgym

goal
getting

planning for
non-planners

D0281051

Free
password for
The Mind Gym
Online with
this book

Here is your personal password to become a
member of The Mind Gym Online. To join, simply visit
www.themindgym.com and enter this code.

TNBU CF14

The verdict on
'The Mind Gym: wake your mind up'

Winner of The MCA Management Handbook of the Year award, 2005.

Press

'Success without the sweat ... of practical use not only at work but also at home' *Financial Times*

'Fashionable salons are buzzing with a new kind of drug, and it's called intelligence ... '*The Mind Gym: wake your mind up*' is at the top ...' *The Sunday Times, Style magazine*

'The Mind Gym is a book that teaches you how to use your brain in new ways ... Definitely something to think about' *Independent on Sunday*

'Inventive about techniques to deal with everyday situations' *The Times*

'Read The Mind Gym. It's full of mental exercises to stop you functioning on autopilot' Dear Deidre in the *Sun*

'Everyone who is anyone in business seems to be talking about this book. 10/10' *Irish Times*

'What could be smarter than having a personal trainer for your brain?' *Evening Standard*

'It's time to indulge yourself - make sure you're equipped with the most luxurious accessories to fit every corner of your life ... The Mind Gym is no. 1' *Eve*

'Brainy ideas to get your grey matter into fifth gear' *Harpers and Queen*

'One chapter and you'll take over the world' *Image*

'Life-changing ... Accessible, fun and fascinating' *Woman and Home*

'Business book of the week' *Money Week*

'The usual hogwash' *Private Eye*

People

'If every business leader applied the techniques in this book, the UK productivity gap would disappear in a moment' **Tim Melville-Ross** CBE, Chairman of Investors in People, former Director General of Institute of Directors

'Revelation, revelation, revelation - I love The Mind Gym for all its helpful tips that I use every day and make my life so much easier and more enjoyable; a really super invention' **Kirstie Allsopp**, Presenter, *Location, Location, Location*

'Whatever jungle you are doing battle with, The Mind Gym's tips and techniques are highly likely to give you the confidence and skills to come out victorious' **Dr Sandra Scott**, Psychological Consultant on *I'm a Celebrity, Get Me Out of Here!*

'To stimulate, order, de-stress and ultimately secure peace of mind, whether for personal or professional use, this book is a bedside necessity which you can rely on for the best advice' **Emilia Fox**, Actress

'This is the perfect intelligent and intuitive guide for everyone who wants power, wealth and influence - without bloodshed' **Simon Sebag-Montefiore**, author of *Stalin: The Court of the Red Tsar*

'This is my kind of gym: you can do it wherever you like, you see the benefits immediately, you're never bored and no communal showers' **Richard Reed**, Co-founder, innocent

'Finally, a way to unlock the vast amount of our brain capacity that we all have but few of us ever use, my mind feels more toned already - I love it!' **Sahar Hashemi**, Founder, Coffee Republic

'Got any sense? Want some more? Join The Mind Gym' **Nick Jones,** Founder, Soho House clubs

'When it comes to improving our minds, The Mind Gym is the number one brand - you can trust it completely and may even fall in love' **Rita Clifton**, Chairman, Interbrand

Professors

'The best psychology turned into neat ideas for living smarter. Credible, imaginative and practical: you can't ask for more' **Professor Guy Claxton**

'I am very impressed by the intellectual rigour and academic integrity of this immensely enjoyable and practical book' **Emeritus Professor Peter Robinson**

'Filled with everyday uses for some of the best psychological research of the last fifty years, this is a must for anyone who is serious about making better use of their mind' **Professor Ingrid Lunt**

'Packed with helpful directions for people struggling with the challenges of daily living, The Mind Gym puts the new positive psychology into practice and offers a multitude of ways to live a strong and healthy life'
Professor Michael West

'This is a very well written and well researched book packed with good advice, useful tips, accurate self-assessment questionnaires and helpful practical exercises. It contains 10 times as much information as its rivals and is neatly packed into nicely formed bite-sized pieces' **Professor Adrian Furnham**

the mindgym

give me time

TIME WARNER
BOOKS

TIME WARNER BOOKS

First published in Great Britain in January 2006
by Time Warner Books

A CIP catalogue record for this book
is available from the British Library.

ISBN 0 316 73169 2

Typeset in Avenir by M Rules
Printed and bound in Great Britain
by Clays Ltd, St Ives plc

Time Warner Books
An imprint of
Time Warner Book Group UK
Brettenham House
Lancaster Place
London WC2E 7EN

www.twbg.co.uk
www.themindgym.com

The Mind Gym ran the first 90-minute workout, a fast-paced, face-to-face workshop filled with practical ways to use our mind better, at Deutsche Bank on 1 September 2000.

Since then:

- 66 different workout subjects have been developed including 'Getting things done', 'Saying No', 'Dynamic delegation' and '90 minutes per hour'

- over 100,000 people have taken part; 92% say they have used what they discovered in the workouts when asked a few weeks later

- 360 organisations have run workouts, ranging from the BBC and London Business School to Virgin, Microsoft and BP

- the workouts have been delivered in 5 languages in 27 countries by qualified Coaches based in the UK, US, Australia, Ireland, France, Spain, Italy and Austria

The Mind Gym Online, which was launched in January 2005, has 30,000 members.

But that's just figures

Those who have been to the time related workouts have a wealth of tales about what they've done differently as a result. 'When talking with stores on the phone I now take longer and listen to all their concerns first. They are then much more cooperative,' explained one. 'My first half hour at work was relatively unproductive. Now I know it's my most alert time of the day I use it for the difficult things which means I get them done faster,' recalled another. 'I've stopped worrying about the work/life balance and started enjoying both a lot more,' enthused a third.

'I'm a convert . . . the stickiness of The Mind Gym learning is extremely impressive,' declared Steve Crabb, industry expert and editor of *People Management*. 'What Fosbury did for the high jump, The Mind Gym has done for learning,' exclaimed Dr Bill Lucas when Chief Executive of the Campaign for Learning.

The Mind Gym's Academic Board of four psychology professors (all Fellows of the BPS and one past President) ensure that The Mind Gym's content has integrity and is up to date. One way that they do this is judging The Mind Gym prize for new research-based insights on how we can use our mind more effectively - the latest thinking on thinking, if you like.

'The Mind Gym: give me time' is packed with many of the most popular hints, tips and techniques from the workouts and is The Mind Gym's second book (the second in a series from Time Warner Books). For information on all of this, and plenty more, visit www.themindgym.com.

Contents

Give me time   1

I don't have time to read this book   7

Time signature

Ⓐ Hawks and doves   23

Ⓑ My kind of time   32

Ⓒ Time warp   46

Ⓓ Rushaholics   55

Ⓔ Concentration curve   67

Ⓕ Mañana   77

Time well spent

Ⓖ Joy division   89

Ⓗ Pathfinder   103

Ⓘ Goal getting   113

Ⓙ Planning for non-planners   123

Taking command

Ⓚ Over-committed   139

Ⓛ Dead time   150

Ⓜ Interruptions   156

Ⓝ Persistent offenders   165

Ⓞ Saying No and being loved for it   172

Ⓟ A quick read   182

People power

Ⓠ Fleeting meetings   207

Ⓡ Off load   221

Ⓢ Getting time with time poor people   230

Ⓣ Toxic time cultures   239

The beginning of time   250

References   260

Index   265

Without whom   270

Give me time

The problem of not having enough time is almost as old as time itself. The Roman philosopher Seneca was writing about it in AD49. He even devoted a book to the subject: 'On the shortness of life'.

Two thousand years later, there are enough manuals, workshops and websites offering advice on how to get more done in less time to fill every waking minute. And still we're not satisfied.

This suggests either that there isn't a solution - dissatisfaction with time is part of the human condition - or we need to find another way of tackling it.

The Mind Gym offers another way. A way that differs from much of the traditional time management advice in at least four significant respects.

Time well spent

The aim of this new approach is to make us feel good about time, both how much we've got and how we spend it.

The search for 'enough time' is, alas, futile. For many of us, no sooner do we have enough time than we come up with a host of exciting new projects that we want to do and, hey presto, we don't have enough time any more. This is entirely healthy. Any attempt to restrict our imagination and appetite for new adventures seems quite wrong. Equally, it does mean that we are destined never to have enough time (or enough imagination). We can see this as a pain or, like the fact there is only one ace of spades in a pack of cards, an integral part of the game of life. Either way, having 'enough time' is not a helpful goal.

What is worth seeking, when it comes to time, is satisfaction. Or even better, time that delights.

Give me satisfaction

Secondly, rather than focusing on ways to be more efficient, this new approach presents three keys to feeling good about time: control, immersion and purpose. Each of these has the power to unlock some time delight; combined together they are virtually unassailable, the nearest there is to a guarantee for time well spent.

Control

Of all full-time workers, those that are happiest about the balance between work and the rest of their life, are, surprisingly, the people who work the longest hours: the self-employed. This apparent paradox is explained by a simple yet vital finding: the more we feel in control of our time the better we feel about how it is spent.

Immersion

Happiness is a state of mind that occurs most often when we are immersed in what we're doing. It may be trekking in the Himalayas, fighting to get to the next mission in 'Grand Theft Auto' or painting a watercolour. It doesn't matter what the activity is. What does matter is that we feel sufficiently stretched and excited by what we're doing to be completely engaged. On these occasions, we are far more likely to feel that our time is well spent.

Purpose

Our greatest satisfaction comes when we believe that what we're doing matters. This may be because the specific activity helps us to realise a personal ambition: to be appointed head teacher, to perform in a concert. Or we may see it as contributing to something larger: to help children succeed, to give people pleasure.

One size fits no one

We each have our own time DNA. As a result, what helps Jack may be a hindrance, or even damaging, for Jill.

Whilst a little planning helps some people feel much better about how their time is spent, it is a source of unbearable constraint for others.

A third distinction of The Mind Gym's approach is that it cherishes our differences. And so, instead of the orthodox approach which tries to get us to shift from 'A' - our current unsatisfactory way of behaving - to 'B' - the guru's magic formula - The Mind Gym aims to shift people from 'A' to options.

As a result, there are stacks of questionnaires and other tools to help you spot your individual time preferences and proclivities. And plenty of guidance about how to use the results to discover which remedies are most likely to work for you and which ones you'd be better off avoiding.

The intention is to make us more aware of our options and more informed about their implications, not to force-fit us into a single template.

Solid as a clock

There is a mass of brilliant psychology, which, were we to know it, would make our lives unimaginably easier. Unfortunately most if it is hidden away in academic tomes and journals that are impenetrable to all but the most intellectually minded. At the other end of the spectrum, there is an apparently limitless supply of self-help and company training which is easy to digest but often based on little more than the perceived wisdom of the author.

The fourth distinction of The Mind Gym's approach is that it draws the most useful elements from both, often adding a new twist.

Time is a subject where this approach is particularly useful. Academics are largely dismissive of traditional time management tools. Some have even conducted experiments to test the effectiveness of these time-honoured techniques and found that they had no demonstrable impact on their efficiency and performance compared with those who hadn't taken part.

The populists, on the other hand, are either unaware of, or have chosen to ignore, what the independent research has uncovered about human beings and how they relate to time (eg, My kind of time, chapter B).

The intellects and the populists, it would appear, could not be further apart. And yet both have valuable insights. Bring them together and we arrive at a new way of looking at an old subject.

For example, in chapter M (Interruptions) the unintentional chain reactions our behaviour causes, as characterised by renowned psychologist Eric Berne, is combined with some more of the populist tactics for dealing with interruptions. The result: how to change what you do today to reduce the interruptions you will have days, weeks or even months down the road.

Only where there are no relevant sources are the techniques entirely new and even then they are still based on solid psychological principles.

The Mind Gym beliefs

The Mind Gym's approach to time, as with the approaches to other subjects, is based on the following assumptions.

- We choose how we think. We are not pre-programmed to see the world in a certain way but are largely free to decide how we think and how we communicate.

- We can all improve. Rather like a physical gym where we can get fitter, we can find ways to become more mentally capable and more satisfied with how we spend our time.

- We tend to underestimate the extent to which what we do is habitual, using mental 'default settings' that we set ages ago and have forgotten we can change. By discovering more of the options that are available, it is easier to escape our current habits or 'settings'.

- There is sometimes one default option that is better than the old one. For example, a technique that enables us to read faster and increase comprehension is more useful than one that is slower and less thorough (see chapter P). But different circumstances require different approaches so, overall, it is more helpful to keep a range of options in mind.

The purpose of this book is to help us become more aware of our time habits and so make more informed decisions about whether and how to change them.

So, no prescriptions, just a plethora of well tested tools and techniques from which to pick and use.

Does it work?

The tips, tools and techniques in this book have all been tested amongst the 100,000 people who have taken part in The Mind Gym workouts. If these participants considered them practical and useful, not just at the end of the workout but when we came back to ask them weeks or even months later, then they are included. If they weren't helpful then they aren't here.

The book has also been scrutinised by The Mind Gym's Academic Board of psychology professors - all Fellows of the British Psychological Society and one a past President. As a result, any hint of hokum has been vigorously weeded out.

What now?

The next chapter is called 'I don't have time to read this book'. If that's how you feel then that's where you should head. It has a questionnaire to guide you to the chapters that you are most likely to find helpful.

Equally, feel free to flick through the chapter summaries (p. 18) and pick out what appeals. There is no prescribed sequence and no need to read from beginning to end. Your time is too precious for that.

Tick, tock.

I don't have time to read this book

Reading this book from cover to cover is unlikely to be the best use of your time.

Some of the chapters may be extremely helpful but others could be entirely irrelevant. If you don't go to many meetings you won't get much value from chapter Q, Fleeting Meetings, and if you're already a skilled delegator, you won't need the hints in Off load (chapter R).

So, here are some ways to get what you need, with speed.

Read a chapter that appeals to you and leave it at that

If you simply want some practical guidance on how you can turn down a unappealing invitation without offending your oldest friend, then just go straight to the relevant place (Saying No and being loved for it, p. 172). Or you might be looking for a cure for being over-committed (p. 139), or wondering how to assert yourself against a culture of long and wasteful working hours (Toxic time cultures, chapter T). The chapter summaries on page 18 will tell you where to find what you are looking for. Like a book of short stories, you can dip in and out as you like.

Read a section

The chapters are grouped into four sections each with a different focus.

- **Time signature**
  What's your relationship with time and how could it be better?

- **Time well spent**
  Doing the right thing is as important as doing things right. This section focuses on making sure that valuable time is well spent.

- **Taking command**
  Here you will find tools and techniques to make sure that you are in charge of how your time is spent.

- **People power**
  Our time is often wrapped up in other peoples'. If others are involved in your time trials, this is the section for you.

Each section starts with a brief overview about what you will find inside.

Adopt a programme

Follow one of the programmes outlined on pages 9-10. Rather like a fitness workout designed for strength or stamina, each of these programmes has been developed to help address a specific goal.

Design your own programme

There is a questionnaire on pages 11-13 that can help you decide which chapters are most likely to help you address your current priorities. The questionnaire is also available online. Fill it in and use the results to create a tailor-made programme.

Of course, if you prefer, you can always start at the beginning and read straight through to the end. This is your gym for you to use as and when you want.

The Mind Gym Online

The Mind Gym Online is open 24/7. It's a place to practise, prepare, share and, if you want, compete. In the Mind Gym Online you can:

- complete the questionnaires and get a more in-depth explanation of your results. You can also send the questionnaire to friends and colleagues and discover how their views fit with your idea of yourself.

- access specific tools to help you prepare and revise your own plans.

- share ideas and seek advice from other, like-minded members of The Mind Gym.

- keep a private record of how you are doing, the details of your personal goals, and anything else you'd rather no one else knew about.

And more goodies are being introduced all the time in response to what members want and use. To start your membership of The Mind Gym Online, simply visit www.themindgym.com and enter your password which is on the inside front cover of this book. And if you're already a member simply add this code to your existing profile to unleash a treasure trove of new online experiences.

Wherever you see in the book, there's something at The Mind Gym Online that is directly relevant. But if you don't have access to a computer, don't worry, everything you discover in these pages makes complete sense without any further support.

You now know all you need to get going. If, however, you would like to follow a particular programme, or design your own, read on.

The Mind Gym programmes

Here are three programmes that have been developed to help you get what you want from 'The Mind Gym: give me time' as quickly and efficiently as possible. After all, time is of the essence.

1 Free me up
For people who know what they want to do but never seem to have enough time to do it.

2 Happy days
For people who are doing lots but aren't getting much pleasure from it.

3 Pest control

For those who find that other people are their biggest problem.

See pages 11-13 for these routes.

Give me time - Free me up

For those who know what they want to do but never seem to have time to do it.

Time signature

Hawks and doves		23
My kind of time		32
Time warp		46
Rushaholics		55
(E) Concentration curve		67
Mañana		77

Time well spent

Joy division		89
Pathfinder		103
Goal getting		113
Planning for non-planners		123

Taking command

(K) Over-committed		139
(L) Dead time		150
(M) Interruptions		156
(N) Persistent offenders		165
(O) Saying No and being loved for it		172
(P) A quick read		182

People power

Fleeting meetings		207
(R) Off load		221
Getting time with time poor people		230
Toxic time cultures		239
The beginning of time		250

Give me time - Happy days

For people who are doing lots but aren't getting much pleasure from it.

Time signature

(A) Hawks and doves 23

My kind of time 32

Time warp 46

(D) Rushaholics 55

Concentration curve 67

Mañana 77

Time well spent

(G) Joy division 89

(H) Pathfinder 103

(I) Goal getting 113

(J) Planning for non-planners 123

Taking command

Over-committed 139

Dead time 150

Interruptions 156

Persistent offenders 165

(O) Saying No and being loved for it 172

A quick read 182

People power

Fleeting meetings 207

Off load 221

Getting time with time poor people 230

Toxic time cultures 239

The beginning of time 250

Give me time - Pest control

For those who find that other people are their biggest problem.

Time signature

Hawks and doves 23

My kind of time 32

(C) Time warp 46

Rushaholics 55

Concentration curve 67

Mañana 77

Time well spent

Joy division 89

Pathfinder 103

Goal getting 113

Planning for non-planners 123

Taking command

Over-committed 139

Dead time 150

(M) Interruptions 156

(N) Persistent offenders 165

(O) Saying No and being loved for it 172

A quick read 182

People power

(Q) Fleeting meetings 207

Off load 221

(S) Getting time with time poor people 230

(T) Toxic time cultures 239

The beginning of time 250

5 steps to design your own programme

Step 1

Fold the section of page 15 to the right of the dotted line back on itself so you can see the circles on page 17 (but nothing else on that page).

Step 2

Complete the questionnaire on page 15. Look through each of the statements that begin 'I wish that' and pick the option that is closest to your view. There are five options:

1   This is already largely true or it's not that important to me.
2   This would be nice to have but there are other things I'd prefer to have first.
3   Yes please. This would be great.
4   Wow. That would be absolutely fantastic. How soon can I have it?
5   I'd give my right arm for this.

In order to get a good idea of where to start, try to give a range of scores across the different statements. If everything gets a 5 then you will be none the wiser.

Step 3

Transfer the score for each question to the chapters that are suggested on page 17.

Step 4

Add up the scores for each chapter and write them in the Total score circles. The chapters with the highest score are the ones that you should probably focus on. You are now equipped to design your own programme.

Step 5

You could, for example, start with the chapter with the highest score and then move on to the one with the second highest score and work down your list (where two chapters have the same score, start with the one that comes earlier in the book).

Alternatively, you could calculate your average score (say 7) and develop a programme with all the chapters that scored over 7, starting at the beginning of the book and working through.

If you complete the questionnaire online you can print out a bookmark with your personal programme which will make it even easier to stay on track.

Design your own programme

I wish that ...

	already largely true	nice to have	yes please - great	absolutely fantastic	give my right arm
I felt happy about how my time is spent	1	2	3	4	5
I had enough time to do the things I wanted	1	2	3	4	5
My time was my own	1	2	3	4	5
I wasn't so busy	1	2	3	4	5
I could get the same result for less effort	1	2	3	4	5
I wasn't always rushing	1	2	3	4	5
I had more time to think	1	2	3	4	5
Managing time was easier	1	2	3	4	5
I was able to concentrate more	1	2	3	4	5
I felt productive throughout the day	1	2	3	4	5
I got everything done	1	2	3	4	5
I did more of the things that I want to do	1	2	3	4	5
I felt more excited about what I was doing	1	2	3	4	5
I felt a greater sense of accomplishment	1	2	3	4	5
I had more of a plan	1	2	3	4	5
I was better at dealing with time wasters	1	2	3	4	5
I had less to do	1	2	3	4	5
I didn't waste so much time	1	2	3	4	5
I was interrupted less	1	2	3	4	5
I had more time to myself	1	2	3	4	5
Some people didn't take up so much of my time	1	2	3	4	5
I didn't suffer from information overload	1	2	3	4	5
My meetings were more productive	1	2	3	4	5
I spent less time in meetings	1	2	3	4	5
I could get others to do things for me	1	2	3	4	5
I got to see people who don't want to see me	1	2	3	4	5
I found it easier to get time with busy people	1	2	3	4	5
People around me used my time better	1	2	3	4	5
Managing time was more in my nature	1	2	3	4	5
I didn't have to check things off with so many busy people	1	2	3	4	5

Fold this portion of the page back on itself and write your score directly into the relevant circle on page 17.

Time signature

(A) Hawks and doves $\quad\bigcirc+\bigcirc+\bigcirc=\bigcirc$

(B) My kind of time $\quad\bigcirc+\bigcirc+\bigcirc=\bigcirc$

(C) Time warp $\quad\bigcirc+\bigcirc+\bigcirc=\bigcirc$

(D) Rushaholics $\quad\bigcirc+\bigcirc+\bigcirc=\bigcirc$

(E) Concentration curve $\quad\bigcirc+\bigcirc+\bigcirc=\bigcirc$

(F) Mañana $\quad\bigcirc+\bigcirc+\bigcirc=\bigcirc$

Time well spent

(G) Joy division $\quad\bigcirc+\bigcirc+\bigcirc=\bigcirc$

(H) Pathfinder $\quad\bigcirc+\bigcirc+\bigcirc=\bigcirc$

(I) Goal getting $\quad\bigcirc+\bigcirc+\bigcirc=\bigcirc$

(J) Planning for non-planners $\quad\bigcirc+\bigcirc+\bigcirc=\bigcirc$

Taking command

(K) Over-committed $\quad\bigcirc+\bigcirc+\bigcirc=\bigcirc$

(L) Dead time $\quad\bigcirc+\bigcirc+\bigcirc=\bigcirc$

(M) Interruptions $\quad\bigcirc+\bigcirc+\bigcirc=\bigcirc$

(N) Persistent offenders $\quad\bigcirc+\bigcirc+\bigcirc=\bigcirc$

(O) Saying No and being loved for it $\quad\bigcirc+\bigcirc+\bigcirc=\bigcirc$

(P) A quick read $\quad\bigcirc+\bigcirc+\bigcirc=\bigcirc$

People power

(Q) Fleeting meetings $\quad\bigcirc+\bigcirc+\bigcirc=\bigcirc$

(R) Off load $\quad\bigcirc+\bigcirc+\bigcirc=\bigcirc$

(S) Getting time with time poor people $\quad\bigcirc+\bigcirc+\bigcirc=\bigcirc$

(T) Toxic time cultures $\quad\bigcirc+\bigcirc+\bigcirc=\bigcirc$

Transfer your score for each question into all the relevant circles on the opposite page (16). When you have finished there should be a number in each circle. For example if you scored 4 in the first question, put a 4 in the circles on the opposite page (16) in the row for (A) Hawks and doves, (C) Time warp, (G) Joy division and (H) Pathfinder.

A,C,G,H	○
A,K,O	○
C,O	○
C,D	○
J,R,P	○
D,J,K	○
D,L	○
A,B,F	○
E	○
E	○
F,M	○
H,F	○
G,I	○
G,H,I	○
J	○
Q	○
K,O,R	○
E,I,L,P	○
M	○
L,N	○
N	○
P	○
Q	○
Q,T	○
R,T	○
S	○
S	○
B,M,N	○
B	○
S,T	○

A summary of each chapter

(A) Hawks and doves

Being satisfied with our time is largely a matter of choice. Find out if you're making the right ones.

(B) My kind of time

Does your work time drag and your play time fly by? Find out how you may be tricking yourself into wasting time.

(C) Time warp

Different personalities benefit from different time saving techniques. Find out which ones will suit you best.

(D) Rushaholics

Get more done by speeding up. Right? Wrong. Find out when slowing down gets you there faster.

(E) Concentration curve

Discover energy saving devices to ensure that your mood maximises your minutes.

(F) Mañana

Why put off doing today what you can put off doing tomorrow? This chapter cracks the procrastination code.

(G) Joy division

The best times are happy times. Discover the elusive and sometimes surprising sources of joy and so how to make the good times great.

(H) Pathfinder

It's no good doing the right things if we're heading in the wrong direction. Use these techniques to chart the right course for you.

(I) Goal getting

'It was great - time just flew by.' Find out how to get more moments when you think you're time couldn't have been better spent.

(J) Planning for non-planners

A chapter for those who put planning on a par with cough mixture and only just above going to the dentist. There is a better way.

(K) Over-committed

So much to do, so little time. What to do when we've written cheques we have no hope of cashing.

(L) Dead time

Delays, jams and stops. How to regain the time you thought you'd lost.

(M) Interruptions

Some interruptions are welcome. Many are not. Find out how to get more of ones you want and none of the ones you don't.

(N) Persistent offenders

It is said once is a mistake, twice is a pattern and three times is a habit. This chapter deals with those who make a habit of abusing our time.

(O) Saying No and being loved for it

An essential tool in the day-to-day battle for control of our time. Find out how to use it to maximum effect.

(P) A quick read

Allegedly, the world's store of written information doubles every four years. Here's a way to keep up with the new material.

(Q) Fleeting meetings

Meetings: good or bad? With the techniques in this chapter, you decide.

(R) Off load

How to get someone to do it for you, right, first time.

(S) Getting time with time poor people

How to get time with people who think they don't have time for you.

(T) Toxic time cultures

How to save time when all around are wasting it and blaming it on the way we do things here.

The beginning of time

What's a good use of time and what's not? This chapter provides the tools to help you make the tough calls.

Time signature

If you were sitting in the psychiatrist's chair you might be asked about your relationship with your father. Don't worry, that won't happen here. Instead, this section is going to delve into a relationship that's murkier, as deep rooted and rarely talked about, even behind closed doors: your relationship with time.

It's unique, it's personal and once we understand our own individual take on time we can discover whether we'll ever think that we've got enough (A, Hawks and doves); could gain by planning less (B, My kind of time); have unidentified pleasures lurking at work (C, Time warp); need to slow down or speed up (D, Rushaholics); would benefit by leaving important things to later in the day (E, Concentration curve); or could achieve more by demanding less (F, Mañana).

You already know your pin code, your mother's maiden name, and maybe even your blood type. Now, uncover your time signature and with it the ability to match the right time enhancing techniques to your unique time style.

(A) Hawks and doves

Will you ever have enough time?

It may seem like a daft question. Who knows what the future will bring? But stick with it - there is a way that you can look into a crystal ball and predict the future with a high degree of accuracy. And it isn't difficult. Just answer this question:

Do you have enough time now?

Whether you answered yes or no, that's also likely to be the answer to the first question about the future. Because it's not to do with the number of hours we have available, or the amount of work we have on: our sense of whether we have enough time is to do with how we think, and specifically how we think about time.

In the same way as people see the glass as half full or half empty (or the wrong sized glass), by choosing to think differently we can transform our feelings about the same objective facts.

In short, if you have the right attitude to time you have a very good chance of being satisfied, not only with how much time you've got but also how you spend it. But if you don't, you will find it extremely difficult to feel either of these things, however hard you try.

Have you got what it takes?

We tend to underestimate the extent to which we choose how we think. Just because we were once pessimistic doesn't mean that we always have to be a pessimist. Once we become aware of how we are thinking we can take control and make changes to our outlook. Similarly, if we want to alter how we look at the world or, in this case, time, it's good to have a fix on how we're thinking already.

To get a sense of how you consider time, complete this short questionnaire. For each pair of statements, pick the one that is closest to your view. If neither seems quite right, pick the one that seems least wrong. Don't leave any questions out.

If you're concerned that someone might see your copy of the book, there is a confidential version at The Mind Gym Online.

	A	B
1	I like having everything done	I like having things still to do
2	I'm frustrated that I can't do everything I want to	I'm excited by having to choose between lots of options
3	Not having enough time is annoying	Not having enough time is a sign of a fulfilling life
4	I wish I had more time	I wish I made better use of my time
5	If I had enough time to do everything I'd be happy	If I had enough time to do everything I'd come up with more things to do
6	Time is against me	Time is on my side
7	I feel frustrated by how much I have to do	I feel exhilarated by how much I have to do
8	I'm always looking for ways to do the same thing faster	Once I've got a routine that works, I tend to stick to it
9	If you give me more to do I'll find a way of doing it	If you give me more to do I'll have to drop something else

10 There are almost always ways of being more efficient	Sometimes that's just how long it takes and there's nothing you can do about it
11 I constantly look for opportunities to hand over assignments to other people, even if it may be risky	I am generally better off getting on with things than trying to find someone else to pass them over to
12 I frequently revisit my priorities to make sure that I am still doing the right thing	Once I've decided on a course of action I tend to keep to it
13 Better to keep trying short cuts even if they are sometimes dead ends	Better to get on with what you know will work rather than run the risk of ending up back where you started
14 Keep searching for a better way	Do what works

The explanation behind your answers will be revealed in a few pages.

Are you busy?

Some of us like to be busy.

Of course, we may pretend otherwise: 'I just don't have a choice; if I could find a way of not having to do all of this, I would.' 'Do you think I enjoy having so much on?' But what if the time fairy waved her wand and suddenly removed all the arduous activities that we didn't want to do?

Before you could say 'grandfather clock' we'd have found a whole load of new things to do. And what would we say then? 'I'm too busy, I haven't got enough time'? Probably.

For many busy people this crazy business is part of their identity. If you removed all the things we had to do, we'd find a whole lot of new ones. Not because we are masochists but because this is what makes our lives exciting and keeps us motivated.

The saying, if you want something done give it to a busy person, rings true precisely because busy people like having a lot on. This may also be one of the ways in which they maintain their self-esteem (see chapter K - Over-committed).

There is nothing wrong with being busy. In fact, there are many advantages. Busy people tend to

- do the things that will have the greatest impact. Economists refer to the Pareto principle which suggests you get 80% of the benefit for 20% of the effort. See chapter K for more on this.

- achieve more and be happier because the pressure they are under motivates peak performance. That said, too much pressure can have the opposite effect and bring things to a frenetic halt. (It is called 'flow' - you can read more about it in chapter I - Goal getting.)

- lift the mood, motivating people around them and stimulating even the idlest folk into action.

So being busy, rather than being a sign that we haven't got enough time, may actually be a sign that we are using our time well. But does this make us feel any better about the amount of time we have?

Busy means happy

Some of us are perfectly happy about having more on than we can possibly achieve.

We recognise that, whatever the magazines claim, we aren't going to have enough time to run a bank, bring up our children, venture off on romantic escapes, learn three languages, write award winning novels and do our bit for charity. We not only accept that it is impossible to find time to do everything but that being faced with this panoply of possibilities may be a source of energy and excitement.

People who think like this are Time Doves. They recognise that making difficult choices is an unavoidable consequence of life.

Yes, they might muse, it would be lovely to have lots of parallel lives, say one for romance, one for family, one for special projects and so on. But this isn't going to happen. Time Doves treat choice as a challenge - they aim to pick out the best bits and combine them, rather than being frustrated that they can't do everything.

Busy means misery

Others, however, don't have such a laid back attitude. We read the same magazines about how to have it all, and are deeply frustrated.

These people are Time Hawks. For them, making choices about how to spend their time isn't exciting, it's maddening. How, they argue, can I possibly be satisfied with a situation

And still not enough hands

where I won't be able to do all the things that I want to do? Fair point. There is nothing wrong with this argument except the out-come: Time Hawks have set themselves up to be constantly dissatisfied with the amount of time they have.

Time Hawks are forever facing dilemmas. Should they try out the new restaurant or see a movie? Work out, go clubbing or get a good night's sleep? Take a Spanish lesson or invite their cute new neighbour to a salsa session? They will always feel unsatisfied at having to make a choice between two appealing alternatives. It's no good, they sigh, I just don't have enough time.

No matter how many time saving techniques they discover, Time Hawks will never feel that they have enough time. This is their destiny.

There is more than one kind of dove (and hawk)

It doesn't stop with separating the hawks from the doves. There are differences within each species. Imagine these two views.

1   Sure, there isn't enough time to do everything. I'll just use what I've got as best I can.

2   I know there will never be enough time but I am going to make sure that I get the absolute best out of every minute I have got.

Both these views come from time doves: they are both content that they will never have enough time. But they are very different types of dove.

The first is a resigned dove. People with this view recognise the inevitability of not being able to do everything and so carry on doing whatever they can manage in the time that they do have. If they had a theme song it would be 'Que Sera, Sera'.

The second is a striving dove. They also readily accept that they will never have enough time to do everything they want, but they believe that there are ways in which they could get more out of the time they've got. As a result, they keep on searching for short cuts, willing helpers and other methods to get more done in less time.

It's the same with hawks. There are striving hawks, always eager for a way to be more effective. And there are resigned hawks, resigned to being buffeted by the dictates of the clock.

It isn't all black and white, of course. There are degrees to which people are striving or resigned but for the sake of simplicity, let's consider the four primary views on time. These are summarised in this table.

	Hawks	Doves
Striving	Destined always to be frustrated that I don't have enough time but still striving to find ways to get more of it.	Happy that life is full of choices, and that I won't ever have enough time to do all I want; but still striving to find ways to make better use of the time that I have got.
Resigned	Destined always to be frustrated that I will never have enough time. I have given up trying to do much about it.	Happy that life is full of choices, and that I won't ever have enough time to do all I want. Relaxed about doing what I can in the time available.

What am I?

To find out if you are a hawk or a dove, look at your answers to questions 1-7 in the questionnaire above.

If the majority of your answers were A then you are a likely to be a hawk. If the majority are B then you are probably a dove.

To find out if you are striving or resigned, look at your answers to questions 8 to 14. If you answered mostly As you are probably striving. Mostly Bs and you are likely to be resigned.

	Mostly As	Mostly Bs
Questions 1-7	Hawk	Dove
Questions 8-4	Striving	Resigned

You should now have a clear idea which type of time bird you are.

What should I do about it?

Whilst none of these alternatives are wrong, there is one attitude that gives us the best chance of having a good time: the striving dove. With this attitude we don't get frustrated that we can't fit everything in and we keep on searching for ways to make better use of the limited time that we do have.

If you already have this attitude, congratulations. You are likely to enjoy the rest of this book which is packed with tips, tools and techniques that will help you get more of what you want in the time that you've got. More importantly, you are on the right track to having a good time and a good use of time.

But what if you have one of the other time attitudes? Does it matter, and what, if anything, you do about it?

Turn me into a dove

What's wrong with being a hawk? Nothing. So long as you don't mind the fact that you will never feel that you have enough time; at least not without a major change in your life, like retiring, and quite possibly not even then.

For those hawks who would like to be doves, here are three techniques to help you cross the species.

1 Ask yourself what's the benefit of remaining a hawk? Given that dove-like thinking means that you can feel good about the

amount of time you have and hawk-like thinking means you can't, the pragmatist, the utilitarian and the pleasure seeker will have little problem swapping sides.

But what if you think that doves are wrong? What if you believe that it is possible to have enough time to do everything, or at least everything that you want to do? Try the next exercise.

2 Imagine your perfect day. Fill it with all the things that you most want to do - money no object. Maybe it starts with a champagne breakfast on a terrace overlooking the Mediterranean and then a gentle massage followed by a swim in the sea with a delicious fitness coach. Fill the day exactly as you would like, with the right amount of time for everything.

Next, imagine that you get a call from a friend. Johnny Depp / Uma Thurman / Nelson Mandela / Ellen McArthur (or whomever you would most like to meet). They are in the area and would really like to come round and see you. What do you do?

If you agree to see them then you can't do one of the things that you had planned for your perfect day. And if you don't agree to see them then you are missing out on a great opportunity. You have no option but to make a choice and, in doing so, recognise that even in the perfect day there isn't enough time to do everything.

However well you organise your life or build your skills at dealing with time, unless you have fairly limited aspirations or are incapacitated, you won't have enough time to do everything you want. It's logically impossible. You can get in a sulk about this - or you can celebrate that your life is rich enough for there to be lots of choices. This latter view is the way of the time dove.

3 'Life is a game but bridge is serious,' was the joke on the back of a set of playing cards. Whether you share this enthusiasm for bids and rubbers or not, treating life as a game can help move our thinking towards a more dove-like perspective.

If you played Monopoly with a limitless supply of cash then it wouldn't be much of a game. Poker would lose its thrill if every card was the Ace of Spades, as would Scrabble if every piece was a blank. What makes these games challenging and enjoyable is that the resources are limited.

This is the same with life. And whilst some people start with certain advantages - a great brain, fabulous legs, a sizeable inheritance - we all have the same amount of time. It is the great leveller. The game or challenge is about using it to best effect, so no point getting upset that we don't have enough. That would only ruin the game.

Strive alive

The danger of being resigned is laziness. We do what fits relatively easily into the time we have but, because we don't make the effort to find simpler, neater ways of achieving what we want, we miss out.

If you want to become more of a striving dove or hawk, review what you have done today. What could you have done differently that would have enabled you to achieve the same amount in less time? Are there conversations that you could have cut short? Did you search for your keys only to discover they were in front of your nose? Did you get lost going somewhere? Or agree to something that you didn't really want to do? Did you have an argument with your computer? Or with a friend?

Write down five ways that you could have saved time today. If you can do that then there are lots of ways you can make better use of your time tomorrow.

The rest of this book is full of practical suggestions about what we can do to spend more time doing the things that we most want to do.

And if you are worried that all this reading is going to take too long, go first to chapter P - A quick read. For Hawks and Doves alike this will help you get through this book faster and get back to your life quicker.

So, what are you waiting for?

(B) My kind of time

When rail travel first arrived in Britain it brought with it its own kind of time. Previously, local areas had calculated time from the position of the sun at midday. As a result, time varied across the country. When the new telegraph technology enabled all railway stations to receive a standardised time signal, trains began to run according to London Railway Time. However, this varied from the local time - in some areas by as much as fifteen minutes. To try to deal with this stations had two clocks, one showing local time and another showing railway time.

The situation was finally standardised with the introduction of the rather magnificently named 'Definition of Time' bill. Now our station clocks show the same time as our watches, as do the displays on our televisions, our mobile phones, microwave ovens, games consoles and laptops. And because we all describe time in the same way, we might assume that we all experience it in the same way - but we don't.

Not all hours are equal

Like our preference for brown or white bread, we don't all like our time served the same way. In organisations and groups we see these different preferences expressed in attitudes to punctuality (does it matter?), deadlines (set in stone or simply something to keep the boss quiet?), diaries (essential tools or a nice piece of stationery?), action plans (love 'em or leave 'em?) and so on. What is a matter of great importance in one place is scarcely given a second thought in another.

In the same way, as individuals we each have a time preference. Finding ourselves in a job - or a relationship - that doesn't suit our style can be deeply frustrating. Equally, being somewhere or with people who suit our strengths is likely to be uplifting and time generating. And, even better, we can also borrow some helpful behaviours from alternative time styles and so get the best of both worlds.

Seeing into the future

A simple way of looking at time styles is to gauge how much we want to predict or control what is going to happen. In the meticulous blue corner we have the planned people, eager to anticipate and comfortable with certainty. In the red corner, where the paint is still wet, are the spontaneous types who relish ambiguity and delight in exploring the unknown.

If you and I go on a holiday we might well see the preferences in action. I want to know where we're staying each night; you want to see what's available when we get there. I want to check out train timetables, pre-book restaurants and map out the route; you're happy to be guided by your mood and whatever opportunities crop up. By day three we're driving each other nuts. Let's hope this isn't our honeymoon.

Neither of us is right or wrong but perhaps we shouldn't be travelling together. That said, maybe I could experience a few more adventures if I adopted some of your flexibility - and you might get some more good meals if you'd just book a table for two at eight thirty.

The above scenario is, of course, a simplification. Just because we favour a style in one particular situation doesn't mean we operate that way in all situations. A spontaneous traveller might be extremely well planned in their work, and someone with a preference for well planned holidays may run their social life around last minute impulses. That said, research does suggest that we all lean more strongly to one preference than the other. Working in a way that fits with this preference we are more likely to perform at our best. And when we're forced to operate within a different kind of time style we are more likely to feel pushed out of shape and at a disadvantage.

Planned

People with this preference tend to be at their best when things are:

- ordered. I know what needs to be done.
- prepared. I've got a plan.
- definite. And I'm sticking to it.
- thought through. I've anticipated any surprises.
- in control. I know what's happening and when.
- structured. Every project needs a plan.
- familiar. I have a pretty clear idea about what's going to happen.

Planned people enjoy organising. They are likely to be punctual, unlikely to cancel and they'll remember your birthday - it will be in their personal organiser, which they will have remembered to back up. They don't like to be rushed but once they've made a decision they'll stick to it.

They are at their least comfortable when a situation is ambiguous and they hate plans that keep changing.

People with a preference for being planned are well suited to organising groups and taking care of detail. They thrive in organisations with well defined processes and are terrific at keeping plans on track.

Spontaneous

People with this preference tend to be at their best when things are:

- changing. I love it when new things turn up.
- flexible. My plans are in pencil.
- casual. I like to keep my options open.
- last-minute. Now? Why not?
- open. Don't worry, you don't have to commit just yet.
- new. It's different so let's try it.
- ambiguous. Who knows where this might lead?

They tend to be energised by the imminent approach of deadlines (and less upset when they whoosh past). They get excited by changing plans, are quick to make decisions and can be equally quick to change them. They may well be fervent channel hoppers and are likely to be reading several books at the same time.

They are at their least effective when they have to follow a plan. And they dislike it when they can anticipate what the future will bring.

People with a preference for being spontaneous are well suited to jobs where flexibility and thinking on their feet is important. They keep cool when faced with the unexpected, indeed they enjoy it.

A summary of the differences

	Planned	Spontaneous
Plans	Love 'em. Milestones, dates, responsibilities. This is the way to get things done.	No thanks. Anything more than a to-do list hurts. Plans will change so why plan?
Changes to the plan	Not keen. I'd prefer to stick to the plan we agreed on.	Yes please. I'll change tack at the slightest suggestion.
Distractions /interruptions	Loathe 'em. Focus on one thing before moving on to the next.	Love 'em. Give me energy as I move in and out of different projects.
Decision -making	Considered. I like a clear process to gather the relevant information. Once made, the decision holds.	Quick - I can always change if circumstances require.
Time keeping	Precise. I see it in blocks.	Ambiguous. I see it as a flowing stream.
Meetings	I like a pre-circulated agenda - and I like to stick to it.	Not very keen on the word 'agenda'. Prefer to let the meeting find its own way.

Approach to getting more time	Find ways to be more efficient. Better sequencing and work flow; process improvements and shortcuts.	I go and do something else that will deliver the same or better result. I don't get stuck in a rut, I just move on.
What it is like working with them	Reassuring. If they say they'll do something they will. Can be quite rigid.	Can be thrilling. You'll never be quite sure where you stand. They may intend to do one thing but end up doing something completely different.

What am I?

You may well have spotted your time preference already. If you are unsure, complete this questionnaire.

Choose one of the following options.

1 When something unexpected means I have to change plans, I

   a   feel annoyed by a break to my programme

   b   like the idea of doing something a little different

2 Keeping to a plan

   a   is frustrating

   b   is satisfying

3 I like to decide what I do socially

   a   well in advance

   b   at the time

4 I like my life to be fairly

a   consistent

b   unpredictable

5 I think that

a   variety is the spice of life

b   better the devil you know than the devil you don't

6 Dull activities are best

a   done in one go

b   interspersed with more interesting activities

7 I like to

a   make quick decisions

b   mull over the options

8 I work best

a   swiftly at the last minute

b   methodically and steadily

What type are you?

Mark your scores against the list below.

Planned	1a, 2b, 3a, 4a, 5b, 6a, 7a, 8b	Total =
Spontaneous	1b, 2a, 3b, 4b, 5a, 6b, 7b, 8a	Total =

Can I be both?

Although we may sometimes move between the two styles, it is likely that we favour one over the other.

However, if we don't see the strengths of our time style we may not make the best use of it. Spontaneous people who have attended too many time management sessions are sometimes led to believe that their flexibility is a weakness, rather than a strength. Similarly people with a planning preference sometimes come to the conclusion that this indicates a lack of creativity on their part. Neither is true.

A rush of blood to the head

Sometimes the environment in which we are operating may prevent us from identifying our preference. This is what happened in the case of Mike, a workout participant.

Mike was sure that he had a preference for planned but the questionnaire suggested otherwise. Initially, he was confused by this but after some discussion the apparent contradiction was explained.

At 16 Mike had run away and joined the army. His new world proved to be a very welcome break from the unpleasantness he'd left at home. As the army had, as he saw it, rescued him, he understandably saw everything to do with the army as good and adopted many of their mores as his own.

The army puts enormous value on being planned and organised and relatively little, at least for a new Private, on being flexible and spontaneous. As a result, he presumed that he liked order.

In fact, by remembering the elements of his childhood that he had enjoyed, and the time in civilian life when he felt most at ease, he realised that his real preference is for the spontaneous approach. As a result, he not only understood why he wasn't enjoying things that he'd thought he should enjoy, but he is now able to choose roles and relationships that are likely to make him both more effective and happier.

Try doing it their way

As we have seen, to feel satisfied with the use of our time we need to choose roles and activities that suit our time style. But it can also be valuable to borrow habits and behaviours from the other preference. Sometimes this is necessary; to fit in with the style of a project team, perhaps. Other times it is useful;

spontaneous people often find indulging in a little pre-planning creates opportunities for freewheeling later on. But whatever situation we find ourselves in it is helpful to develop our reper-toire to the point where we can pick and mix to make the very best use of our time.

How multi do you task?

Some people like to weave in and out of different projects whilst others prefer to complete a task fully before moving on to the next. Orthodox time management teachings encourage us to complete one thing before starting the next. But is this right? Are these multi-taskers really less effective?

The anthropologist Edward Hall examined how different cul-tures treat time in different ways and developed a scale to illustrate the different ways that people handle their time.

At one end of his scale he placed monochrons: people who like to do one thing at a time and make sure that they've finished it properly before going on to the next.

He put at the other end of his scale highly polychronic people. They love dipping in and out of tasks. They read a few pages, make a phone call, tidy something away, come back and read a few more pages, reply to an email, and so on.

Three other psychologists (Kaufman, Lane and Lindquist) then went on to ask whether the amount we naturally multi-task (ie, the extent to which we are polychronic) makes any difference to our level of stress and, by implication, performance. They chose as their source dental surgeries. The research showed that, in the case of dentists' assistants, their inclination towards sequen-tial or multi-tasking made no difference to their stress levels. With the dentists themselves they found a different result: the more polychronic they were, the less stressed they became in demanding situations and the greater their job satisfaction.

Further research by Allen Bluedorn adds support to the hypoth-esis that it is easier to excel at more sophisticated and complex roles if you prefer doing several different things at the same time. Polychrons for President?

Quick fixes for harassed Planners

- When faced with a change of plan, try to welcome it rather than fight it. See the new direction as an advantage that may bring fresh energy or make the eventual outcome richer, rather than an obstacle to be overcome.

- When you make a plan, think of it as a relatively loose collection of activities that may well change for the better, after all, no one has 20/20 foresight.

- When you're running late and there's nothing you can do about it, let go of the worry. Instead, consider what you can do in future to avoid a repeat.

- Keep your eyes and ears alert for new opportunities - curiosity may have killed the cat but for most humans it's how we find the hidden ingredients that save us time.

- If you're going to miss a deadline, don't panic. Get on with doing what you can do in the time left; it's often more than we imagine.

- When someone suggests an alternative, listen without judging. It may save you time and pain, but you'll never know if you dismiss it before they've finished talking.

- If things are getting stuck or going wrong, re-evaluate your goal. There's nothing wrong with changing direction if a better opportunity comes along.

- Remember, some of the best deals are last minute.

There's plenty to be gained by borrowing attitudes from our spontaneous cousins including less tension, greater opportunities and more ideas. Today's great leaders are valued at least as much for reacting fluidly to changing circumstances as for having a great plan in the first place.

Quick fixes for disorganised Spontaneous types

- For even a reasonable sized project, make a plan. It doesn't have to cover every detail and you don't have to stick to it but at least you will have a clearer idea of the scale of the challenge. And it will help other people know what to expect too.

- Do some research before you start. It will get your unconscious mind thinking about the subject, which may well help later.

- It can pay to stick with the original plan even if you've thought of something better. Check that the effort of changing, not just yours but everyone else's, is sure to be justified by the benefit of your new approach.

- Think back to when you've wasted time because you didn't think ahead. Is there a pattern? If you always forget something when you go away overnight, then a checklist in the bathroom cupboard could be a valuable time generator.

- When the outcome really matters, do yourself a favour and get organised beforehand. Are you sure your partner will forgive you if you toast your anniversary with cheap wine from the petrol station (for the third year in a row)?

- Finish things. A job half done is a lot of effort wasted.

- Look for what you can do now that will make tasks swifter in future. A filing system for emails, an envelope for receipts; don't just tidy up the bedroom but arrange your clothes so it will be easier to get dressed in the morning.

However enjoyable it is being spontaneous, there are many times when borrowing attitudes and behaviours from the planners pays off handsomely, even if it hurts.

With a fair wind

Josh loves sailing and he is a planner. When he sails, he gets out the charts and plans his route. He knows where he is starting from and where he is going to and how he intends to get there, but he has to allow some flexibility for the changing winds and sea.

At work Josh tends to plan in great detail. As a result he runs out of time when things don't go according to plan and finds this stressful. When considering what he could learn from the Spontaneous people, Josh realised that he could apply his sailing philosophy to his working day. Interruptions, last minute requests and changes of plan are like the sea and the wind: unpredictable but inevitable and part of what makes the challenge exciting. If he could handle them at sea, he could surely manage them on dry land.

Other people's time styles

Once we have identified our own time preference, we face another challenge: how to cope with friends, lovers, colleagues and clients who have different preferences where, inevitably, there is the possibility of disagreements and misunderstandings.

One enlightened workout participant told how she launched an imaginative rescue plan when she noticed that time preferences were putting her relationship under strain. The problems arose over how to spend the weekends. She hated her boyfriend's pre-planned schedule and he was equally unhappy with her unpredictability. She could feel herself getting bored, whilst he complained that he felt under pressure to fit in with her plans at the last moment.

Their solution was to have alternate weekends: planned and spontaneous.

On the planned ones he fills the diary with commitments and people to see. Recognising her appetite for spontaneity, he keeps this to himself and lets her discover what's planned as the weekend unfolds.

On the spontaneous weekends she comes up with some last-minute trip to an unusual place. Knowing he likes a plan, she gives him a place and a time to meet: 'Under the clock at Paddington, 6pm sharp and bring your walking boots.' 'At least this way he thinks I have a plan,' she explained. Maybe.

Being similar can cause tensions too. A participant recalled what happened when her son was born.

'Up until then we had both been fairly carefree. At the weekends we loved nothing more than jumping in the car and just driving into the country. And during the week we would rarely organise our nights out more than a day ahead. Then Tom arrived. Suddenly there was an enormous amount of administration and planning to do. He [the father] carried on much as before. He was always happy to help, but I was the one who had to organise the nappies, the nurseries and all the medical checks.

'At first I was furious but then I worked out why. I was being forced out of my time preference and he was not. We talked about it and, I am delighted to say, the admin burden is now being shared.'

Team time styles

If mismatched time styles can cause friction in a relationship, what happens when we put a whole team together? A group of people with the same time preference would certainly have its advantages - it would be easier to reach agreement, at least about how things were done.

But there would be serious risks.

A team made up exclusively of planners would find it difficult to cope with a change in deadline or a redirection of the project. Equally, in a team full of spontaneous types there is a good chance of a last-minute panic, and effort may be wasted as they change direction along the way.

The most effective teams have people with each preference. And there is sufficient respect on either side for the respective strengths to be used to maximum advantage. The planners do the planning but resist going to the level of detail that will restrict the spontaneous thinkers. They may set the agenda for team meetings but they are not inflexible; they allow the group to explore new issues that arise during the discussion.

It's a different matter when it's the boss or client who is on the other side of the time divide. One of the most consistent complaints about managers is based on conflicting time preferences. Either they keep changing their mind or they don't seem to trust anyone.

If you're a boss who suspects some time style friction in your team, this might be an opportunity to reassess - how many of them share your time preference? And what about those who don't? Could you be making better use of their different approach to time?

If, however, you are working with a manager or a client whose preference is causing you problems, you need strategies.

One option is to accommodate. Show them plans, charts and detailed budget estimates if that's what it takes to keep them happy. Or, if they're forever changing their mind, try to see the strengths of their approach - embrace their suggestions and find ways of incorporating them into your plan. For more on this, see chapter S, Getting time with time poor people.

Alternatively, you could try to temper their spontaneous enthusiasms. For more on this see chapter N, Persistent offenders.

So, what's the secret?

The secret lies in being aware.

Once we understand time preferences and know our own, we can:

- appreciate our strengths whilst realising that we haven't got it all.

- look for roles and a lifestyle that suits our preference.

- identify where we'd be better off by borrowing from the other preference.

- value the differences in our colleagues, lovers and friends and find ways to use these to make our relationships stronger.

- adapt to suit the time preference of people we want to impress or get on with.

Give your mind a workout

I SPY See if you can spot the time preferences of the people you live and work with.

Here's a checklist of the types of thing you might spot people with each time preference saying and doing.

Planned	Spontaneous
Prefer to reach conclusions	Prefer to leave things open
Like finishing things	Like starting things
Appreciate warnings and don't like surprises	Relish adapting to last-minute changes
Have a view and communicate it clearly as if it is fixed	See views as tentative and always open to being adapted
Frustrated by side discussions and meetings that go off the agenda	Happy to get side tracked on to an interesting subject

Planned	Spontaneous
Assume there is a 'right' thing and try to stick to it	Make no assumptions about what is right and go with the flow
Overlook new things in order to finish the current job	Put off current tasks to investigate new opportunities
Make decisions quickly and look for closure	Postpone making the decision and look for options

I TRY If you want to identify places in your life where borrowing from the other preference would be useful, try talking to someone who has that preference.

 If you'd rather do this with someone you don't already know you can find suitable partners when you log on to The Mind Gym Online and use the LikeMinds search facility.

(C) Time warp

In 2002 a painting by one Jan van den Hoecke was found to be wrongly attributed. Relabelled as a Rubens its financial and artistic value shot up, transforming it from a £500,000 minor work to a £49 million masterpiece. Our time may not carry that kind of price tag but the labels we put on it can have a similarly dramatic effect on how we perceive the value of what we do with it.

And it doesn't always go the way of the Rubens; the label we choose is just as likely to make us discontented and frustrated as deliver a time windfall.

A trick with mirrors

When lifts were first introduced into high-rise buildings many people had a complaint. The damn things were too slow. Rather than call the engineers in for a redesign, a quick and easy solution was found: put mirrors on the wall. Once people could fix their hair instead of twiddling their thumbs, they were just fine. Their lift journey took the same amount of minutes but now they had been given the opportunity to label their ride as 'me time' their problem was solved.

Similarly, just by changing the labels we use we can become much more fulfilled and delighted with how our time is spent.

Label 1: Work

Imagine for a moment that you are asked to complete a simple task, say, working on a puzzle. Now imagine that you are told that you are also going to be paid for the time you spend on the task. How would that affect your attitude? Would the fact that you are being paid as well make you feel more positive or less?

Value in the label?

Psychologists tested exactly this scenario under experimental conditions. One group received a dollar for working on the puzzle and the other group were unpaid. In the results they found that the group who received no money not only worked at the task longer, but also reported having enjoyed themselves more than the paid group.

'Work', it would seem, is less pleasurable than 'play', even when it is in fact the same activity. What it comes down to is the label that we put on it.

You've got to laugh - or not

Harvard psychologists Ellen Langer and Sophia Snow set out to investigate whether people experience an activity differently depending on whether it is called work or play. Participants in the study were asked to sort a pile of Gary Larson cartoons in three different ways, with varying degrees of complexity.

Even though the cartoons were humorous, those participants who labelled the more complex task as 'work' enjoyed it less than those who had the label 'play'. The 'work' group also found that their minds wandered twice as often.

Work to live or live to work?

Steve loathed washing up - at a guess, he's not alone with that feeling - but he decided to accentuate the positives. Elbow deep in warm, soapy water he acknowledged that doing a repetitive task gave him a well needed space in which to think. He also mused on the fact that it could be viewed as a sensual experience and, being something of a process freak, he began to develop a system for making the task more efficient. It would be going too far to say that he now enjoys washing up, but refusing to see it as a chore certainly made him less resentful of the time he spent on it.

A similar transformation happened to Margot who loved living on the eighth floor of a groovy city centre apartment block - until the lift needed replacing. Ten weeks of slogging up and down eight flights of stairs were anticipated as a painful waste of time, until she renamed it a workout and took to the stairs with a poetry book. Two months later she'd dropped a dress size, learnt six of her favourite poems and made friends with a whole new set of neighbours. It never stopped being tough on her thighs but, like the lift passengers with their mirror, labelling the time as a personal benefit made the long climb a lot easier to face.

If some of our negative feelings about work are indeed coming from the label rather than the task itself, then a little rewording could lead to a significant shift in our experience.

Put life into work

The work/life balance is a popular concept that goes something like this: a happy life is one where 'work time' and 'life time' are in balance. However, for many people the balance is weighted towards the work side and this has a negative effect on the life side. The answer lies in correcting the balance.

It sounds neat, and for people in conditions of chronic work induced stress it is a useful and important exercise. But for others, who may be simply bored and frustrated, it can make the dissatisfaction worse. As we've seen, uttering the word 'work' can turn good times bad. Add to that the suggestion that our work is depriving us of our life and no wonder we're feeling grumpy.

The alternative is to relabel our work activities. Here are four ways to do this which will enhance your time on the job.

1 It's not work

Make it work for you. What do you enjoy doing in your leisure time? Where at work can you get a similar buzz? If you're a social animal who likes parties then running meetings or networking across different business areas could fit the bill. Or if you're planning a second career as a novelist then drafting those reports could be good train-ing - after all, someone else is paying you to polish up your writing skills. And sales calls are a gift for trainee scriptwriters with an ear for dialogue.

2 I'm getting better

'Experience is a good teacher but she sends in mighty big bills,' said the US writer Minna Antrim. Good, bad or indifferent, every day teaches us something new. Reflect on it. Write it down, keep a jour-nal; it could be the raw material for a creative project; it could help prevent you making the same mistake again; it could lead you to a new business theory or a stand up comedy routine. John Grisham was working a 70-hour week in a small US legal firm when a case on which he was working inspired him to start writing.

3 Give me the good stuff

Don't just wait for the great jobs to come to you. Decide on what you could do that you'd find enjoyable or stimulating then go and volunteer for projects that appeal. Put yourself in the fast lane if that's where you want to be.

4 My labels, not yours

Do it your way. Don't let the pessimism of others ruin your day. We all get pleasure out of different things. Just because the guy on the next desk hates sales promotion, doesn't mean that you can't get a thrill out of closing a deal.

Conclusion:

Don't save your pleasure for your leisure. Any time that feels rewarding is good time. That can happen at work just as much as anywhere else.

Label 2: 'My time isn't my own'

Our lover wants to spend time with us and that's fine; if it's the den-tist that's less good. But in both these cases, we have control. We can say no to the lover if we want to, and we can ignore the dentist's reminder card. But there are other situations in our lives where we feel we have less choice and some occasions when we feel we have no choice at all.

A group of PAs who took part in The Mind Gym workout agreed when one of them complained, 'Time tactics are no good to me. I can't control how my time is spent.' Their role was to be reactive, not proactive. Or so it seemed until they tried the following exercise.

They were each given a sheet of paper with a line down the middle. On the left they listed all the time munching things they considered to be outside their control. On the right they challenged the statements they had made, writing down anything they could think of that might influence those 'uncontrollable' factors. To their surprise they came up with a long list. Instead of using the slightly quieter times to recover could they use the time to prepare resources for the next onslaught? And rather than waste time reworking reports, why not design a briefing form and get all the information signed off up front? Once they got the hang of it, the group identified a whole variety of areas where they could set boundaries, contribute suggestions, seek out information, set up processes that would get them on the front foot and save them time later on.

Who's your puppet master?

At the root of our feelings of lack of control over time there is often an unhelpful assumption about who is pulling our strings. When we believe that events in our life are determined by factors outside ourselves - by fate, luck or other people - we have what the psychologist Julian Rotter describes as an 'external locus of control'. If, on the other hand, we believe that we are running our own show, we are described as having an 'internal locus of control'. People with an internal locus have greater job satisfaction, they recover from illness more quickly and report leading more fulfilling lives than those who believe their strings are pulled by others.

Our assumed locus of control is generally considered to develop in childhood. Those with highly controlling parents are more likely to have an external locus of control, whilst those whose parents encouraged activities where their children could see the results of their efforts (developing a musical skill, for example) tend towards an internal locus.

How we perceive the locus of control in our lives is just that, it's a perception. It's not fixed. It's up to you.

As a result of the exercise the group of PAs reconsidered their opinion and realised that a significant amount of their working time could be labelled as their own. They would, of course, still be called upon to react to emergencies and last-minute requests but, just maybe, that was part of the attraction of the job: 'I quite like fire fighting,' said a participant, 'just not all the time.'

And if, having gone through this exercise, they decided that they did find these limits unpalatable, they could consider giving up being a PA and set about finding a job that had greater autonomy. Over that decision, they agreed, they had total control.

Over to you

This is the grid used by the PAs (it is also available online with prompts). Use it to discover what you can do to increase control over a time consuming area of your life.

Choose a person, or an event that you feel is dominating your time; it might be a work project, a family member, a study commitment or a business schedule. In the left-hand column list all the elements over which you feel powerless. Now, challenge them one by one. Use the right column to record everything that you can think of - at least four actions for every item in the left column. If you suspect that you might be operating with an external locus of control (see box above), you may find this takes a bit of effort, but keep at it. You will surprise yourself with the amount of options you come up with.

Some of the options won't appeal; that's fine. The point is that you develop a range of options that give you control over how you spend your time.

The person or event:

Out of my control	What I can do
	1
	2
	3
	4

Out of my control	What I can do
	1
	2
	3
	4

Conclusion:

There tend to be more things we can do to control how our time is spent than we imagine. As the saying goes: time flies, luckily you're the pilot.

Label 3: Relativity

Whatever we decide to do with our time, we are always making a choice. Doing one thing excludes doing another, different thing. When the choice is easy, it feels OK. Things get a little harder when the choice involves a stand off between what we want and what we need: I want to go to sailing this weekend but I need to do my tax return if I am going to avoid a hefty fine. We tend to be less happy with that sort of choice. It becomes even harder when principles or duties are added into the equation - I want to go join my friends at the cinema, but I feel I must visit my ailing aunt.

Faced with this kind of choice, even an activity that we might otherwise enjoy can turn sour. I would be enjoying my nephew's birthday lunch if I wasn't missing the Wimbledon final. We usually have a good - even admirable - reason for having 'done the right thing' but fretting over what might have been can cause us to feel very unhappy about how our time is being used. The 'enjoyable meal' label has been replaced with a dirty great sticker proclaiming 'This is not what I want to be doing'. What should have been a pleasure has become a chore.

This is another opportunity to check in with our thinking and, if necessary, apply a different label to the activity to make it more palatable. OK, so the tennis lover in you isn't being satisfied but what about the appreciative partner, the doting uncle, the good friend? Recognise how these parts of your identity are being reinforced by your choice, acknowledge it, and even admire yourself for it. Rename the activity as something you find worthwhile or pleasurable and you'll find it a lot easier to let go of the 'if only' thinking. As a result, the time spent will start to feel very much better.

Label 4: Time = Quality

A panel of experts was asked to review two computer programs that produced identical results. The experts were told that program A had taken far longer to write than program B, but nothing else. When asked which they considered superior, the experts consistently chose program A. When asked why, they could give no rational explanation for their choice.

This survey by D Lynne Persing is just one example of the myth that equates quality with the length of time the task takes. If a meal is knocked together in minutes we assume that it will be less good than one that's taken hours to prepare; a quick decision can't be as good as one that arrives after proper research; and an artist who knocks out a picture every six weeks is less of a painter than one who has finessed their canvas over years.

But this sweeping assumption isn't borne out by the evidence. Something we work on for hours may stubbornly refuse to improve - in fact, it may get worse. Most creative people have a story about a piece of work that they couldn't leave alone until they'd tweaked it beyond repair. And, as the writer Malcolm Gladwell argues in his bestselling book *Blink*, split-second decision-making based on intuition can sometimes be more accurate than judgements arrived at after hours of laborious consideration.

Gladwell tells the story of a sculpture that was offered to the Getty Museum in California. The figure, a Greek marble, was said to date from the sixth century BC and, as such, was a highly significant find. Keen to ensure that it was authentic the museum spent more than a year proving that the sculpture was an original, only to have it denounced as a fake by art experts who saw it for just a few seconds. In one swift glance the experts saw, or perhaps sensed, things that months of painstaking investigation had missed. In this particular case, less time was very definitely more.

It is, of course, true that long periods of sustained effort are often rewarded with great results. The problems start when we turn this assumption into a universal rule and apply it in situations where it doesn't belong. Then we run the risk of:

- misjudging quality. Rather like using price as a proxy for value, the time=quality mistake can skew our judgements.

- encouraging people who want to impress us to spend longer on something than is necessary and so waste their time as well.

- failing to innovate, as we aren't motivated to find faster ways to achieve a similar outcome.

- over-preparing and losing our edge. For example, some tutors at The Royal College of Music advise students not to practise a performance piece within three days of their recital as over rehearsal is likely to dull their sparkle.

Conclusion:
Time spent doing something often bares no relation to the quality of the output.

Label 5: The good time manager

The final label deceit is that of the 'good time manager'. The executive with an allotted time slot for every activity looks pretty efficient, and they may well be. But this rigid time keeping often comes at a price. The disciplined time manager may miss out on the corridor conversations that build relationships; he/she won't have time for the meandering chat that leads to an unanticipated insight or the ideas that spill over the allotted meeting time. Colleagues won't turn to them for advice because they don't have time to give it.

A really good time manager does more than just manage their time; they find ways to remain flexible and sensitive to what's going on around them. They have time for the unexpected.

And here's a salutary time management tale to end on. Julie fell in love (briefly) with a busy but highly organised businessman. At the end of each day he would spend half an hour writing a detailed schedule with time slots for each of the next day's activities. Impressed, Julie took a look at the list and found that item number thirty-five read 'make love'. The relationship didn't last.

D Rushaholics

Slow down, you move too fast

We tend to assume that the way to get more time is to speed up. But speeding up can actually slow us down, as anyone who has ever accelerated out of the house only to realise that their keys, wallet, organiser, and baby son are sitting on the kitchen table, knows only too well.

And it's not just our efficiency that is reduced. The quality of the experience suffers too, as we become less aware or 'mindful'. Ever eaten an entire meal without tasting any of it? Closed a novel without remembering a word? Hurrying up doesn't just give us less time, it can also drain the pleasure and benefit from the time that we do have.

For many of us, hurrying is a way of life. Some of us enjoy the buzz that it gives us whilst others are driven crazy by the constant pressure and feel that their lives are speeding up to an unacceptable degree. Either way, there are almost certainly areas of our life that could be enhanced by a little go-slow behaviour.

First, three tales where less haste has helped others save time and achieve more.

1 Take your foot off the gas

You might assume that if you drive faster you will get to your destination sooner. Not necessarily. At least, not if you are on London's orbital motorway, the M25. This was the discovery made by a group of researchers looking at traffic flow.

Drivers on the M25, like most others, tend to accelerate whenever they get the chance and then brake when they hit the traffic queue. In heavy traffic this creates a kind of concertina effect. However, by introducing a slower speed limit on particularly congested parts of the motorway, as they did in 1995, the traffic flow becomes more fluid. Drivers need shorter braking distances and therefore can follow more closely, and because everyone is driving at almost the same speed the concertina effect all but disappears.

People end up arriving at their destination sooner because they are driving more slowly.

2   No time for the gym?

The Superslow movement in the US applies a similar idea to fitness training, promoting a message that all time deprived people have been wanting to hear for years: if you're short of time for your work-out, don't do more - do less. And here's the proof.

In a study held in 1995, 117 participants signed up to a weight-training regime. The participants were split into two groups. One group did their repetitions at what is considered to be a standard rate of 6 seconds, whilst the other did a slower version, taking 14 seconds for a repetition and only managing between 4-6 repetitions per set.

At the end of the eight-week training programme it was the slow group who saw the best results, increasing their average exercise weightloads by 5 pounds more than the standard group.

3   How 3 minutes can save your wallet

Why do patients sue certain doctors?

Is it, as one might imagine, because of their past performance? Maybe the proportion of patients they cured, or their track record with patient mortality, or maybe it was the type of illness that they specialised in?

A study by medical researchers in the US revealed that it wasn't any of these reasons.

The quantitative factor which most accurately predicted whether a doctor would be sued was how much time they spent with their patients. There was an unequivocal correlation between those who had never been sued and those who spent longer with each patient:

on average three minutes more in the consultation than their colleagues who had been sued. The extra time meant that patients felt they were listened to and given attention, rather than simply being 'processed'. As a result they felt more satisfied and less likely to find fault with their treatment.

And the doctors who consulted for longer saved themselves months, as well as fortunes and their reputations, by staying out of litigation.

Are you a rushaholic?

To find out how much you feel the need for speed, fill in the questionnaire below.

State the extent to which you agree with the following:

	Never	Rarely	Sometimes	Often	Always
I like my day to be packed with things to do					
I get impatient waiting in queues					
I often underestimate how long it will take me to do something					
I tell myself to speed up					
I am known for being busy amongst friends and family					
I worry about the next thing I should be doing					
I often have to go back to get something I have forgotten					
When driving to a new place, I set off without looking at directions					
I eat on the move					

	Never	Rarely	Sometimes	Often	Always
I find myself wondering if I am going to be late					
I fail to notice something beautiful until someone points it out					
I get impatient when I watch someone else doing something that I could do faster					
I try to think or do two things at the same time					
I tap my fingers or jiggle my knees					
I finish sentences for other people					

How did you fill in this questionnaire?

If you

- skimmed each question and answered it almost before you'd finished reading it, add 5

- read each question and thought for at least a second before answering, add 3

- Read the question slowly and thought about each answer for at least a couple of seconds before answering, add 1

For all the other questions score as follows

Always	5
Often	4
Sometimes	3
Rarely	2
Never	1

Here's what the scores suggest:

50-80 Harried and hurried

You are a rushaholic and, if you scored in the top half of the scale, you may well be an adrenalin junkie too.

You are likely to feel that you are doing a lot without necessarily achieving a lot or, if you think you are achieving a lot, can't understand why other people don't appreciate it. One of the reasons is that whilst your energy can be attractive in short bursts, living and working with rushaholics every day is exhausting and can be annoying.

You may well be short on sleep and even when you try to relax, find it hard to switch off. You will almost certainly feel tired a lot of the time.

Running out

Feeling constantly harried by commitments, events and circumstances is not a pleasant way to live. Think about how you can slow down. What requests can you say no to? Can you build in some down time between commitments to recharge? Sure, being busy is fun, but when you're late or lost, and feeling battered and beaten, you may feel it's time to trade in for a calmer karma.

31-49 Pause and pace

You are susceptible to becoming a rushaholic but the good news is that you aren't one, yet.

Don't get caught in the speed trap where you assume that by doing things faster you will automatically get more done. Enjoy the times when you are feeling unhurried and pay attention to the times when you aren't. Make sure that you allow yourself time to reflect and relax.

Review any questions above where you scored 4 or more and think what you can do to change this situation.

16-30 What's the rush?

Hurrying is not an issue for you. You may get accused of dawdling every now and then and others may sometimes consider you slow.

Heart throb

Do people who are prone to heart attacks share a particular kind of psychological makeup? That was the question posed by cardiologists Meyer Friedman and Ray Rosenman.

They suggested that people could be separated into two types: Type A and Type B. A person who is showing Type A behaviours will tend to, for example,

- hurry the speech of others
- become impatient while watching others do things they think they can do better or faster
- schedule more activities into less time
- fail to notice interesting and beautiful things around them
- gesticulate when talking
- play games to win, even with children

The alternative, Type Bs, tend to be more relaxed, laid back, patient and composed.

Researchers wanted to understand the effect of being a Type A.

First, they needed to differentiate the Type As from the Type Bs in a sample of 3,000 people. They did this by annoying them. Initially volunteers were kept waiting without explanation and then asked lots of questions about being competitive, rushing and ambition. The interviewers' behaviour was far from polite - they interrupted, confronted and contradicted themselves.

The interviewees were scored more on the way they behaved during the interview than on the interview itself. (Type A and Type B people often gave similar responses.)

These people were then tracked for almost a decade. The researchers found that once variations in diet, age and smoking had been accounted for, Type As have twice as many heart attacks as Type Bs.

Rushaholics are closely related to one aspect of the Type A personality: time urgency. They are not related to other two: hostility and competitiveness, which appear to have a stronger link to the probability of suffering from a heart attack. Phew(ish).

However, as long as you are using your more measured pace to think before you act, enjoy the pleasures around you and give your undivided attention to what you're doing, you're onto a very good thing. Remember, though, that there is a difference between not rushing and grinding to a halt. Be careful not to lose impetus altogether and change up a gear every now and again.

Rushaholics anonymous

Here are some techniques to help rushaholics find a calmer, more productive way. Don't expect them to work immediately. That's half the point.

1 Recognise your quick fix thinking

Sometimes our instincts are strong; we make instant assessments based on gut reactions and we get it dead right. But not always. Sometimes we push ourselves (or allow someone else to push us) into fast decision making when we are not fully prepared. Maybe we feel the need for an instant opinion; we don't have time to get the facts; or we just don't like the uncertainty. As a result, we leap to a conclusion but end up looking slightly foolish.

Action

Evaluate your decisions. When you feel yourself rushing to an answer, do a double-take. Ask yourself, is this an informed evaluation of the situation, or is it just a quick fix? Don't allow yourself to be pressurised into a snap decision, and don't beat yourself up for not having an answer. Cultivate this fluid way of thinking and you will not only make fewer mistakes, you will also make better decisions.

2 Judge and you shall deceive

A friend of The Mind Gym had a job working in an upmarket gallery. Most of their customers visited by appointment and so they were fairly dismissive of people who walked in off the street (in order to discourage visitors, they were made to ring a doorbell first to be let in). When a Japanese lady came to the gallery to look around they quickly concluded that she must be a tourist and ushered her out. The next day they discovered that the lady in question was Yoko Ono on a shopping trip to London.

Rushing to judge causes problems because once we have decided on an opinion we look for confirming evidence. This means that we give greater weight to information that reinforces our initial hypothesis ('All Japanese tourists carry Prada shopping bags') and tend to dismiss facts that contradict it ('This particular Japanese tourist is wearing Yoko Ono's trademark sunglasses'). As a result, our bias increases and we become further and further removed from the reality.

Action

Defer judgement. Next time you meet someone new do not let yourself have an instant view.

Ask questions and listen intently to what they have to say, but do not form an opinion. Only after 15 minutes should you allow yourself to entertain any kind of judgement and even then it should be a vague impression, as if you were looking at their personality through frosted glass. Keep asking questions and keep listening to their answers.

If you change your view as the conversation continues, you are doing well.

Don't be surprised if you find this challenging. Learning to feel comfortable with uncertainty can take some doing.

3 Take pleasure

Hurrying up doesn't just run the danger of giving us less time, it can also reduce the pleasure and benefit of the time we do have.

The Slow Food Movement argues that we destroy the pleasure of food when we rush through a meal and most of us would agree. This doesn't mean that we should always have two-hour lunches, though that might be a nice idea, but that there are occasions when eating slowly means that we will have a more sensory and joyful experience.

Speed reading has many advantages - in the right place at the right time. But if we're reading poetry, or a novel for pleasure, we want to enjoy the language and savour the rhythm. Rushing at it defeats the object of doing it in the first place.

Action

This simple, practical exercise in awareness is used in meditation classes. To do it you need a raisin (or similar dried fruit) and plenty of time.

Start off by exploring the raisin in detail. Use all your senses. Look at it, smell it, touch it, hold it up to the light; listen to it, even.

Then put the raisin in your mouth. Explore the texture and, as you bite into the raisin, be aware of how the texture changes. Do this very, very slowly. Pay close attention to the taste, see how it changes as you chew the fruit. If your attention wanders, bring it back to the raisin. Finally, swallow the raisin and be aware of how long the taste lingers and how it changes as it fades.

In this exercise you have heightened your awareness of the pleasure of eating by slowing down and focusing your attention. You might not want to take every meal at this pace but practising a little mindfulness can enhance our experience of food enormously.

You could also try eating in silence with friends or family. You might feel a little self-conscious at first (and very small children are unlikely to get the hang of it) but, without conversation, you'll soon find your experience of the food intensifies and deepens. Do it with a partner and it can be remarkably intimate too.

4   Alarm call

Most of us have times and places where we are regularly in a rush: when we're getting up in the morning, catching a train, or when a deadline is looming. And once we are in this hurried state it becomes increasingly difficult to snap ourselves out of it.

If we want to put the brakes on our rushaholism we need to spot the rush before it starts and take pre-emptive action. This is difficult to do; after all, once the sense of panic kicks in we're unlikely to say, 'ah yes, I recognise this scary, rushed feeling, I'll just calm down and take it easy'.

What we need is an alarm call that both alerts us to our impending panic and does something to reduce the rush, like the coffee machine that both wakes us up and also makes us coffee. The psychological equivalent is called Anchoring.

Action

- Choose a place or situation where you are inclined to rush, say, getting up in the morning.

- Think of something you are likely to see when you are in this place, say, the shower curtain.

- Imagine that when you see this object you will feel calm, confident, strong, in control. Now close your eyes, relax and imagine coming across this object in your normal rushed state and then, suddenly, experiencing this wave of positive emotions. Repeat this several times. Each time, recall the impending sense of panic that you normally feel followed by the calm feelings that you want to induce when you spot the object.

Next time you see this object you are likely to feel the emotions that you have associated with it. If the effect isn't powerful enough, then repeat the third step making the image and the emotions more vivid and intense.

5   Add 20%

We all tend to be poor estimators about how long something will take us but rushaholics are notoriously bad.

How long does it take you to get into work? Is that on a good day? A bad day? Hurried people are often rushed because they are over-optimistic in their time keeping. They believe that things will be done quicker than is probable, or even possible, and then they have to rush when reality dawns.

Action

Next time you are estimating how long something will take you, add 20%. Then measure how long it actually takes. If you repeat the activity keep timing yourself until you have enough of a data bank to make an accurate estimate. How different is the reality from your original estimate?

If this feels too random, try unpacking the problem. Think through all the steps you will have to take to make something happen. For example, when we are going by car we often forget that we will need to fill up with petrol, buy some lunch, find our keys, ask for directions or stop to check the map. And we may take a wrong turn, get stuck in traffic, be caught in a storm. The more we think through each stage the more accurate our estimate is likely to be.

6   Simple steps

A workout participant recalled how he had problems waking up in the morning and, as a result, would always be rushing to get out of the house. Sometimes he'd forget his watch, or the front door keys, or even to brush his teeth. When his partner moved in it all changed. Miraculously, or so it seemed, the keys were always on the hook by the door, the umbrella was in the stand in the hall, and there was fresh milk in the fridge for his tea. And even though he still over-slept, he rarely felt rushed in the mornings any more.

Action

Life is full of regular, recurring tasks - many of them rather dull. Identify those moments when you frequently feel rushed. Now, design a system which sets things up so you can do the task with the least possible effort next time.

If, for example, you know you are often late getting up in the morning, set things up the night before. This is one time when it can help to slip into autopilot, so establish a routine that means you don't have to think too much. We may not all have a helpful partner to make sure there's milk in the fridge, but that doesn't mean we can't set things up to relieve the pressure.

7   In the now

Hurrying shifts our perspective on time. We start to project all our attention into the future. We think about what we'll do when we're out of the house rather than leave it; getting out of the meeting, rather than reaching conclusions in it; our arrival rather than the journey. This way of thinking can make things worse as we cease to notice what is happening here and now, and our panic increases. It can also be immensely irritating for the people with us when they sense that they have lost our attention.

Indeed some of us live our entire lives in the future, always thinking about the destination rather than experiencing the journey, focusing on the ends and giving ourselves little time to enjoy the means.

When we concentrate on doing what we're doing now, rather than thinking about what's just happened or what we're just about to do, we are likely to be much more effective.

Action

Three ways to get focused in the present:

- Name what you see. Coffee cup, table, cake crumbs, newspaper, greetings card, empty bottle, pad of Post-It notes, cough mixture, phone, stamps and so on. By forcing ourselves to articulate the name of everything we see, we slow ourselves down and ensure that our concentration is focused on the present.

- Imagine you are Hercule Poirot. You are looking for clues: a cigarette end with lipstick, a book the wrong way round on the shelf, a mobile phone with dust on it. Keep all your senses open for something out of the ordinary.

- Focus on what you're doing not what you're trying to achieve. Each sweep of the paint brush rather than a fully painted wall, each repetition as you lift the weight, rather than reaching the end of your exercise programme.

When coming in second puts you in the lead

What do Berkey, Apex, Gablinger and Chux have in common? They were all first to market with their products and now no longer exist. Berkey produced hand-held electronic calculators, Apex video-recorders, Gablinger low-alcohol lagers and Chux disposable nappies.

The successful companies were the ones who came after them and learnt from their mistakes. Think of Casio, Matsui, Kaliber and Pampers or Huggies.

According to Professor John Kay, the only major example of a successful business that was first to market is Xerox with the photocopier. They were also the first with the personal computer and the mobile phone.

(E) Concentration curve

It's not just deciding what to do that helps us get more for our minute, it is also when we do it. Dame Barbara Cartland proclaimed that there was only one time of day for romantic involvement with the more mature man: 'between luncheon and afternoon tea; they're quite useless the rest of the time'.

Whether or not this particular assertion is correct, the idea behind it is both valid and useful. Our energy levels do fluctuate during the day according to our own, personal body clock and so if we match the tasks we do to our moods, we will achieve more in less time.

You say espresso, I say macchiato

As the day begins a queue of droopy, sleepy heads builds up at the coffee counter, all eager for their morning caffeine fix. Try to engage them in conversation and you might get a grunt but not much more until there is at a least one latte between them and the alarm clock. These people will, when they regain the will to speak, describe themselves as 'not morning people'.

Fast forward another seven hours and the coffee queue is building up again but it's a different crowd. These are the people who didn't want caffeine at 9a.m.; they were at the gym or out for a run or up writing a few pages of their novel. This group are, without a doubt, morning people but by mid-afternoon they are whacked and in need of a boost.

Surf the curves

Psychologists call it our concentration curve or chronotype: the pattern by which our concentration levels vary during the course of a normal day. According to the research, some measures of mental and physical performance can vary by as much as 15% depending on when the activity is done. And this doesn't just affect how quickly we can get to the bus stop: a study with professional swimmers found that their time over 100 metres was 2.7 seconds faster at 10 p.m. than it was at 6 a.m. That's one for the Olympic planners to consider.

In theory, this gives us two options: we can change our concentration curve to suit our lives or we can try to organise our lives around our concentration curve. Unfortunately, our biological makeup means that our underlying curve is not for changing. This leaves one option: to work with our curves and play to our strengths.

Is it time for my medicine?

There is an increasing body of evidence that shows that the time of day that we take medicine makes a difference to how successful the treatment will be.

Asthma sufferers, for example, are several hundred times more likely to have an attack at night than during the day. Symptoms of hay fever are worse in the morning than at night.

Doctors, however, are still taught to prescribe equal doses of medication across the course of the day. Physicians working in the field of chronopharmacology are calling for medical training to include education on the daily rhythms of illness and research into time-specific treatments.

The birds and the clock

If concentration is loosely defined as the amount of time we can focus on a single thought or activity, then most of us can recognise how this changes not just by time of day but also by who we are with, what we're doing and whether we had a bottle of wine for lunch.

Irrespective, however, of whether we need to be up early to catch a plane, our body clocks create a 'circadian signal' which divides our day into two distinct periods: a biological day and a biological night. During our biological night our temperature and hormone levels change and we feel sleepy. For some people, this happens earlier than for others because some of us have a longer biological night and, as a result, need more sleep. It's nothing to do with sloth and it's not something that we can alter through force of will.

The challenge is to identify how our biological makeup affects our concentration levels. To help do this, welcome to the aviary of bird clocks.

First up, appropriately enough, is the lark.

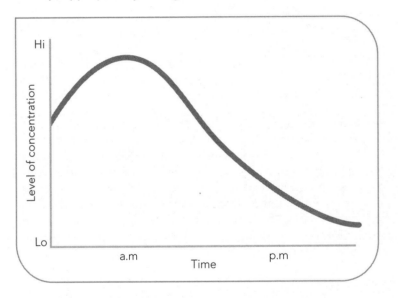

The lark hits the ground running: a 0-60 in 5 seconds; the alarm barely got a squeak out before being silenced. You will have spotted larks, you may even be one - they're the ones with a cheery 'hello' as the rest of the team arrives; they're the school run mothers who've had time to wash their hair. Morning people peak around midday and so, if they're smart, they get the tough stuff out of the way before lunch and leave the afternoon for cruising through more mundane tasks that need less energy and attention. In the evening, they prefer low key activities; morning people aren't clubbers and have no idea what's on late night TV. They'll probably hang on to watch the 10 p.m. news bulletin but by ten thirty the thought of

Newsnight is simply overwhelming. They've wound down so far that there's nothing for it but to set the alarm for 6 a.m. and head for bed.

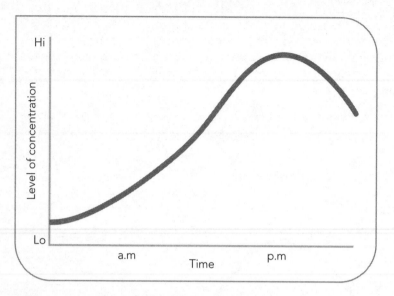

This, by contrast, is the curve of an afternoon person, the one with a longer biological night: an Owl. A slower starter than a morning person - a 0-60 in two hours type - they do function in the first half of the day, but not that effectively. Clued up Owls keep their morning's work simple, in fact they quite enjoy pottering through the boring tasks in that period between cereal and sandwich. By early afternoon they are getting into their stride and are ready to go. This is when Owls take on the hard work. They are at their most productive at 6 p.m. and will probably keep working through till seven or eight, then head out for a full evening. If they're in bed by midnight, they must be ill.

Does the early bird catch the worm?

Researchers haven't found any differences in health, social success or intelligence between the two groups. But there does seem to be a slight difference in wealth.

The later bird may be slower to get started but the worm they catch appears to be bigger and juicier. Before you ditch the alarm clock, be warned, the research is still too patchy to draw any definitive conclusions.

What about me?

Psychologists suggest that only around 1 in 5 of us is a lark or an owl. The vast majority of us are somewhere between the two - described rather charmingly by the researchers as hummingbirds.

This covers pretty much anything that isn't a lark or an owl. It could be that we have a gentle rise in concentration levels during the day peaking around noon, a dip after lunch, and then some recovery through the afternoon and into the evening.

I was born like that

The University of Surrey researchers corralled some 500 people who visited London's Science Museum. In addition to taking DNA samples from their cheeks, the researchers asked them to complete questionnaires about their lifestyles to determine if they were Larks or Night Owls. They did this by asking what time of day they preferred to exercise and how difficult they found it to wake up in the morning. Then they compared the DNA results - specifically the length of the Period 3 'clock gene' - to the questionnaire answers.

The results: 'We found most of the extreme morning preference people have the longer gene and the extreme evening preference people have the short gene,' reported the researchers.

So, next time you're giving your kids a hard time for lazing in bed or staying out late, remember - they probably got it from their parents.

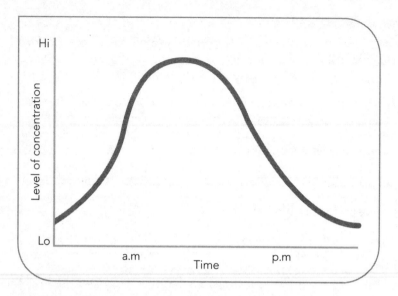

Or maybe, after a rocky start, from mid-morning to the end of the working day is fairly steady, and then concentration slips off in the evening.

One workout participant exclaimed, 'All my low concentration levels are while I'm at work,' before suddenly covering her mouth with her hand, realising the implications of what she was saying.

Tell me why my boss likes Tuesdays

Which day of the week are you at your most productive? A survey for the US firm Accountemps found the following responses from 150 executives: Tuesday 51%; Monday 17%; Wednesday 15%; Don't Know 11%; Thursday 5%; Friday 1%. Getting the most out of our day is great: getting the most out of our week is even better.

From concentration curve to concentration verve

Once we have an idea of what our Concentration Curve might look like, the next step is to re-shape our daily routine to fit it. Some things are fixed, it doesn't make much sense to do the school run mid-morning, but for those activities where we do have a choice, we can now make a decision based on what will make us more productive.

The big match

The most obvious tactic is to play to our strengths, using our prime time for tasks that require higher levels of concentration and our fuzzy periods for activities that are less mentally demanding. Owls would be wise to complete their expenses in the morning; larks, last thing before they go home. And when it comes to crafting a vital email or budgeting for the house move, it's the other way around: larks at dawn, owls in moonlight.

A workout participant who identified herself as a lark, realised that she was wasting the most productive part of her day.

'The first half hour at work was taken up with reading emails, making coffee and flicking through trade magazines. Now I dive straight in and get the work done when I am feeling at my best. I procrastinate less, too, because I know that by the afternoon I'll find the tasks harder.'

The trick is to match our tasks to our mood. So, owls are advised against 9 a.m. job interviews, and larks would probably be better learning Spanish during their lunchtime than at an evening class. But this isn't the only option.

The big mismatch

Another participant at the same workout took a different approach to using her low period in the middle of the afternoon.

'I noticed that if I stayed at my computer I did next to nothing. So, I began to arrange most of my meetings for 3 p.m. Being with other people forced me to stay alert and, by the time the meeting was over, I felt energetic again.'

By deliberately scheduling difficult tasks or meetings in our low concentration periods we increase the pressure on us. This can stimulate us to raise our game and boost our concentration during that sleepy down time. If it works for you it's a great way of kickstarting an otherwise dead part of the day. But it doesn't work for everyone - some people thrive on such challenges, others find them too much.

File under Zzzz

Let sleeping camels lie

Whatever your concentration curve type, if you find you're experiencing a lot more low times than high times, it could be that you're suffering from sleep deprivation. Lack of sleep plays havoc with our circadian rhythms, particularly when it includes a time change. Shift work, for example, has been shown to upset sleep patterns dramatically and anyone who's ever flown long distance knows the brain addling effects of jet lag. Unfortunately, it turns out that catching up on sleep is not as easy as we thought.

In a study on the effects of sleep deprivation, the psychologist Daniel Buysse coined the phrase 'sleep camels' to describe people who work up a sleep debt during the week and then try to make up the time by sleeping longer over the weekend. He discovered that this is a counter-productive exercise as it often requires four nights of oversleeping, and sometimes even more, to reduce one night's sleep debt to zero.

Sleep right

We all know that we need eight hours sleep to keep healthy. But do we? A much discussed US study of over a million people found that those who slept for eight hours or more were 12% more likely to die over the course of the study, whilst those who slept for seven hours had the highest survival rates (having taken into account other contributing factors such as age, diet and previous health problems). Of course, we do sleep longer when we are unwell and this will have had an impact on the result. However, it does suggest that the eight-hour rule is not as clear cut as we have been led to believe.

The team match

We don't just have to look at our own concentration curves. People working in a group will all have their high and low points. When we can match these, everyone benefits.

A normally ebullient team of advertising creatives couldn't figure out why their weekly team meeting was always so flat, however many times they redesigned it. When they looked at each other's concentration curves they had the answer: they were all low at the same point - Wednesday afternoon, the time of the meeting. As a result they moved the meeting and found it was not only a lot livelier as a result, but also more productive.

Give your mind a workout

Part I

Take a few moments to think about your own natural rhythms then plot your curve on the graph below.

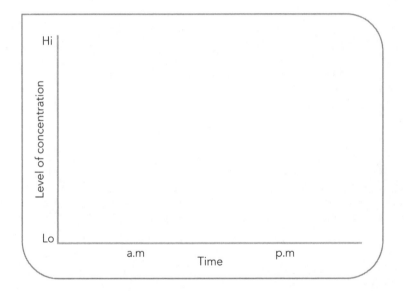

If this doesn't seem quite scientific enough, then record your level of concentration on the hour, every hour for a week, giving yourself a score on a scale of 0 to 10 (where 10 is fully alert). This doesn't need to be complicated, just a page in a notebook or even the back of an envelope. Take the averages across all the days and then you can plot your curve more accurately.

Part II

Answer the following questions and organise your schedule accordingly.

What are the tasks that you regularly do that don't require too much concentration?

What are the tasks that you do that require your full concentration?

How well are they currently matched? What can you do to improve the matching?

When would you want to mismatch, ie, put activities that will force you to be fully alert at times when you naturally have low levels of concentration?

(F) Mañana

Does this sound like you?

'I have loads of great ideas but they don't seem to go anywhere.'

'I seem to start a lot more things than I finish.'

'I have a long list of things that I really must do (and some of them have been around for a while now).'

If these expressions resonate then you are a procrastinator. But you probably know that already. You may have thought about learning some techniques for kick starting yourself but then, well, you didn't get round to it.

Your procrastination habits may seem to be very deep rooted and, indeed, they probably are. But that doesn't mean they can't be changed.

Why can't I get started?

Forget everything you have ever been told about laziness, tardiness, lack of application and short attention span; procrastination is about how we think. More specifically, it is about how we allow certain thoughts to morph into rules. Psychologists refer to these internalised rules as 'beliefs'.

Belief is a big word; it can cover everything from a deep-rooted spiritual commitment to the local double glazing firm's belief in 'putting the customer first'. The beliefs that psychologists are interested in are largely unconscious. They are the hidden motivators, the unquestioned assumptions that drive our behaviour. Think of them as not unlike the operating system that drives your computer - rarely seen or thought about, but very powerful in determining what can and can't be done.

If we are serial procrastinators then we will have some underlying beliefs that are getting in the way of action. And they can pack a mighty punch, immobilising even the strongest motivations and worthiest intentions.

This chapter deals with these kinds of unconscious beliefs - where they come from, how we can identify them and what to do when we've got them. So we can ditch our worst procrastination habits and get more done in less time with no worries. A sort of belief spring clean to help ditch the worst procrastination habits and provide a boost into time efficient action.

Where do beliefs come from, Mummy?

Albert Ellis, a giant of modern psychology and one of the pioneers of Cognitive Behavioural Therapy, suggests that our beliefs are grounded in our genes and shaped by our experiences. We begin life with a predisposition for particular character traits and, as a result, develop patterns of thought which lead to beliefs. But not all these beliefs are equal. Some of them are rational and useful whilst others are irrational and useless, and it's not always easy to spot the difference.

Take the example of Dan, an author. On the surface things were working out well for Dan. He'd been commissioned to write a new book and given a hefty advance that would keep him in laptops for some time to come. The subject was one that was close to his heart, he knew his stuff, and his editor had assured him that the book would sell.

Six months down the line Dan had started to think about what he might wear for the dust jacket photograph and begun practising his signature for the signed copies. Just about the only thing that Dan hadn't started doing was writing the book.

He just couldn't face it. The thought of sitting down and putting finger to keyboard made him feel physically sick. The deadline was looming closer and Dan still had no manuscript. His editor was getting worried and Dan was starting to panic. 'What's wrong with me?' he wailed, over a consoling beer with a friend. 'This should be easy.'

OK, let's stop right there.

Dan was procrastinating, no doubt about it. But why? His dream had come true, he was fully supported by his editor and he was writing about a subject he knows well. The reason for Dan's delay comes in the revelation to his friend, 'This should be easy.'

This is one of those beliefs that the psychologists talk about. It is the primary reason why Dan can't start writing, but it will also have plagued him in many other areas of his life. There are ideas that didn't get off the ground, projects that fell at the first obstacle and relationships that were dropped after a lovers' tiff. In each case Dan didn't get started, or gave up early on, because he has a deep-seated belief that life should be easy and therefore he shouldn't be expected to do things that are unpleasant or hard.

As a consequence, the moment Dan begins to find something difficult, or when he anticipates a problem, he procrastinates. That's what happened with the book. This is why no amount of cajoling, coaching or panicking will get Dan started. To get his fingers on the keyboard, Dan is going to have to change his belief.

Top 10 things we'll start tomorrow, honest

1 Paying the bills

2 Doing the washing up

3 Breaking up with our partner, or sharing bad news generally

4 Writing to thank someone

5 Looking for a new job

6 Getting fit

7 Dieting

8 Getting fit (it's a popular one)

9 Defrosting the fridge

10 Cleaning the car

Right belief: wrong place

Here are seven common beliefs that lead to procrastination. They may sound innocuous or even admirable, and in some contexts they may even be useful. But they can just as easily lead to paralysis. If you find yourself thinking any of these things before you begin a project then you have a sure-fire way of getting more time: challenge the belief.

1 Perfection

It sounds like this:

'It must be perfect'
'I must do it properly'
'It needs to be right'

A desire to succeed: Yes. A desire to perform at our best: certainly. A desire to push the boundaries and break records: great. But a desire for perfection? This is unhelpful. Very little in this world is perfect and in most cases it is hard to know exactly what 'doing it properly' would look like. If we are confident that we can get it right from the outset then it can't be very challenging. Anyway, a partial solution may be closer to what's needed.

2 Certainty

It sounds like this:

'I must make sure I know all about this before I start'
'I want to know what the outcome is going to be before I begin'
'I need to know exactly what will be expected of me before I commit'

Here our intolerance for ambiguity stops us from taking action. We feel as though we will be exposed or that people may discover that we are an impostor and we decide that it is safer to do nothing. Sometimes we try to get more information but with this belief it is unlikely that it will ever be enough.

One workout participant recalled that for years he had been toying with the idea of motorcycling across Europe. Every time the dream got close to becoming a reality he decided that he didn't know enough about the bike, the journey, first aid, the places he'd visit, the local languages or any of a host of imponderables. He told himself that more research was needed. His belief that 'I must be certain' prevented him from making a start.

If everyone thought like this there'd be no Edisons, Picassos, Gorbachevs or Paul Mertons; and not many books, films or new medicines either. If you need to play it safe, don't expect a place in the history books.

3 Assistance

It sounds like this:

'I need a hand'

'Someone should help me out'

'I must get some support'

Do you feel that you need to get a second opinion before you start on something? Some of us feel the need to test the water, to collaborate, consult or get advice. Sometimes this may be the smart thing to do, say, when we are doing something that requires specialist expertise. But, let's be honest, most tasks don't. Our advice hunting is a substitute for action. We may even be hoping that the people from whom we seek advice will actually do the work for us. Rather like a child asking for help with their homework, we're looking for someone better equipped than us to take on the task.

4 Immunity from failure

It sounds like this:

'I must not fail'

'I mustn't mess this up'

'If this goes wrong I'm a failure'

This is a very common one. The feeling that, because we are likely to fail, we should not begin. And so not starting provides us with immunity from failure. Waiving this is a big step - but so are the potential rewards.

Successful people in all walks of life have a long history of failure, it's just that we don't hear about it. Like the gambler whose tales suggest they only ever make money, the business leader, politician and actor may massage their past to suggest an uninterrupted flow of successes. But that wasn't how it happened.

And if it doesn't work out this time, the worst scenario, once we've wiped the egg off our face, is that we've learnt a lot. For resilient people, failure is the seed of future success.

5 Freedom

It sounds like this:

'I should be allowed to do this the way I want'

'I won't be told how to do things'

'I'm not going to do things their way just because they say so'

Sometimes we feel that we've been backed into a corner. We don't want to do what has been asked of us but we can't bring ourselves to say no. So instead, we procrastinate. It's a bit like grown-up sulking - if we can't do it on our own terms we just don't do it at all. Karen, a marketing account manager, felt this way when she was asked to introduce a new invoicing system. She didn't like it and thought the way they wanted it implemented was stupid. But, instead of challenging it she just put off doing it. The consequence was a last minute dash, a missed deadline and an upset team.

6 The right environment

It sounds like this:

'My best work happens when I'm under pressure/relaxed/alone'

'I need to be comfortable before I start'

'I need the right equipment first'

Some of us demand a comfy chair. Others want natural light, a constant supply of sugary snacks or a fully equipped studio. Some of us believe we need pressure, or a total lack of it.

The trouble is that we will rarely have exactly the right environment. Deep down we know this but only when we face up to it will we get on with making things happen, even if it is with the wrong pen.

7 Ease

It sounds like this:

'I shouldn't have to do things I don't enjoy'

'If it hurts I shouldn't be doing it'

'Life should be easy and enjoyable'

It's almost the opposite of the Protestant work ethic. Remember Dan, the writer? This was his belief: that it shouldn't be difficult or unpleasant to get what we want.

Losing weight is rarely a pleasure. When we feel after a period of resisting éclairs and custard creams that we deserve a treat, then it is this belief that is kicking in, and that perfect figure is put back another few weeks or months. Pass the jammy dodgers.

Beliefs makeover

The trick to getting rid of unhelpful beliefs is to rethink them.

Albert Ellis, the psychologist we met at the start of this chapter, observed that our beliefs are often absolute and rigid. As a result the demands we make of the world are littered with words like 'should', 'must', and 'have to'. Ellis coined the rather splendid word 'musturbation' to describe these inflexible demands. To overcome our procrastination we need to listen in to these musturbatory demands and then, consciously and deliberately, replace them with instructions that are less obstructive and more helpful. Doing this is a two-step process.

Step one: Replace rigid demands with softer alternatives

Step two: Add a get-out clause

Step one: Replace rigid demands with softer alternatives

Identify the parts of the belief that include the words 'must'/'should'/'ought'. Now replace them with the words 'I'd like to'/'I'd prefer'/'it would be nice'.

Immediately they begin to sound more like friendly suggestions, rather than harsh instructions. Here's what some of the earlier demands would sound like after a makeover.

Rigid belief	Softened belief
I must get a perfect result	I'd like a perfect result
I must know everything about this	I'd prefer to know everything about this
I need help	It'd be nice to have help
I must not fail	I'd prefer not to fail
I should do this on my terms	I'd like to do this on my terms
I must be under pressure	I'd prefer to be under pressure

Just changing the wording of your beliefs in this way may do the trick. You are less likely to stall if you 'prefer' perfection, than if you 'must have' it. Adopt this softer language and you may find your reasons for procrastination evaporate. But just in case they don't, here's step two.

Step two: Add a get-out clause

Having transformed 'I must get a perfect result' into 'I'd like a perfect result' we now add a get-out clause using 'but':

'I'd like a perfect result but if I don't get one it doesn't matter'

or

'I'd like a perfect result but a good result will still be great'

In effect we are minimising the demand. We are no longer setting ourselves up to fail. If we get the perfect result, magnificent, but if we don't, well, we've already decided that it doesn't matter that much.

Putting it into practice

Joe was procrastinating over doing the DIY. When he checked out what he was saying to himself before starting he discovered quite a few beliefs that were holding him back. The most insistent ones were 'I must know everything before I start' and 'I need the right equipment first'. Acting on this demand Joe had built up a library of unread DIY magazines, bought seven different power tools, two spirit levels and something that resembled a thumb screw. When he realised that his belief was at the root of his problem, he challenged it and rewrote it as 'I'd prefer to know more, but it's not essential.' Then he steamed ahead, new wallpaper and all.

Quick fix

Changing our beliefs is essential if we want to procrastinate less, but it isn't easy. So, here are 10 quick fixes. They won't mend the engine but they are good for a jump start.

More challenge

To be motivating, a goal needs to be challenging enough to stimulate our interest but not so difficult as to be demoralising. Too little challenge and we can't be bothered to start, too much and we don't know where to.

A suitable reward

A stroll in the park, a shopping trip to New York or a room with a view in Florence - choose a reward to fit the challenge and that's worth the extra effort.

Penalty points

For some of us the idea of losing something is more compelling than the idea of gaining it. Write a cheque to an organisation you can't bear. If you don't get the task done, post it. Ouch.

Double, not quit

Procrastinators tend to be super-optimistic when assessing how long a task will take - so there's no need to start just yet. We imagine no traffic, a full tank and perfect directions. Double your estimate for how long the task will take. Better get going.

Dive in

Tackle the tough stuff first. After that it will be downhill all the way.

Move

Stand up, change position, go outside; do something to change your mood and your perspective.

The fast set

We adapt our behaviour to fit in with the people around us. If we mix with a crowd of action heroes and heroines, we are much more likely to kick into action ourselves.

Bite size is right size

As the saying goes, you can't eat an elephant in one mouthful. Break the task into small chunks and identify the end point for each bit. Concentrate on one chunk at a time and congratulate yourself each time you finish an element.

Time fragments

Do you feel that you need to have an uninterrupted slug of time - say, between 2 and 3 p.m. - to complete a task? This doesn't need to be the case. Trying using four 15 minute slots instead.

5-minute start

Do it just for five minutes. No more, no less. When the time is up decide whether you want to continue. If you do, commit another 5 minutes to it. Review and then, if you want, another. And another. If you've got this far you'll be motoring.

Give your mind a workout

I TRY Now you have read this section, put yourself in a position where you know you are likely to procrastinate. Try doing the task that you are putting off. Now listen carefully to what you are telling yourself. What demands can you hear yourself making? What beliefs are driving those demands? Write them down. Now write a new version of each one, tempering it to create a softer, less inflexible version of the demand. Add a get-out clause if it will help.

Rigid belief	Softened belief

Time well spent

'If she knew what she wanted, he'd be giving it to her', sang The Bangles. Lucky girl, only she seems to suffer from the same affliction as many of the rest of us: happiness myopia.

The symptoms are: a future that's out of focus, lack of clarity about what would make us happy and a short term approach to pretty much everything.

The consequences can be serious. Not only is the doting lover deeply frustrated but it's all but impossible for the sufferer to know how to spend their own time wisely. After all, if you're unclear on what you want how can you make astute decisions about how to spend your time?

This section provides the antidote. Swallow one chapter at a time and you will know what you want (G, Joy division); where you're going (H, Pathfinder); what it looks like (I, Goal getting); and how to get there (J, Planning for non-planners).

Complete the course for maximum delight.

Ⓖ Joy division

What would make you happy?

Most of us already have some kind of answer. Love, lucre, lazy days on a sun drenched beach with a perfect body (at least lying next to us) appear on many people's wish list. And that's before they even get started.

But are these really the things that make us happy? Or might we, after a few weeks of this heaven on earth, begin to feel unfulfilled, unmotivated and unappreciated?

Plenty of studies show that, once people have a reasonable level of comfort, greater wealth does not lead to greater happiness. People in the West are no happier now than they were in the 1950s, even though their real income per head is three times greater. The same is true across the world: a growth in wealth has no corresponding increase in happiness once a nation's average income reaches $20,000 per person.

There is also no shortage of successful people who, whilst they have all the trappings of a happy life, are only too willing to tell magazines and biographers, as well as their therapists, of the misery and heartache they suffer despite their apparent success.

The source of happiness, rather like the end of a rainbow, is more of a mystery than we first imagine. However, if we want to be sure that our time couldn't be better spent, then it's a rather important mystery to solve. After all, if we don't know what we want then it's going to be all but impossible to decide how to go about getting it.

And if we do know what is most likely to make us happy we can make much more informed and better decisions about how we spend our time.

Where is the happiest place in the world?

The happiest places in the world are, based on a global survey of over 30,000 inhabitants:

1	Australia
2	United States
3	Egypt
4	India
5	United Kingdom

Three steps to heaven

The search for a definition of happiness has occupied philosophers for centuries. But it's only relatively recently that scientists have got in on the act. Psychologist Martin Seligman and the school of Positive Psychologists have carried out extensive research into the subject and their findings suggest that there are three sources of happiness within our reach. Although none is sufficient, each of them can make a vital contribution to the happy life.

Pleasure
This is about generating immediate, positive sensations. These can be caused by sensory activities: a glass of good wine, a delicious meal, strolling in the sunshine, sinking into a warm bath, making love. Emotional triggers can also cause pleasurable sensations: laughing at a joke, the thrill of exchanging a meaningful look with a stranger in the street, the glow triggered by a good memory. The pleasurable life is packed with feel good sensations; they may be short lived but they are highly enjoyable at the time.

Challenge
A challenge is something that stretches us. And whereas pleasure is something that we react to, challenge is an activity that requires us

to act - physically or mentally. The activity involved may or may not give us sensory pleasure at the time, but it is the sense of accomplishment afterwards that provides the warm glow of happiness.

The kind of challenge that is likely to contribute to our happiness may involve

- doing something we are skilled at, or that plays to our natural strengths
- stretching ourselves so that we learn and increase our skills
- solving a tricky problem or challenge
- persisting when the outcome is in doubt

According to eminent psychologist Mihaly Csikszentmihalyi, the kind of happiness that we get from achieving a challenge is greater than the passive quick hit experiences described as pleasure.

Meaning

Meaning - it's a big word. And, of course, it is different for each of us. Overall, though, it is the sense that our actions are making a contribution to something that we consider to be worthwhile. Like the brick layer who, when asked what he was doing, replied 'building a cathedral', meaning comes from the belief that what we are doing has a value beyond the act itself.

For example:

- Contributing to a social goal, like improving literacy, protecting the environment, or promoting a cause that we consider to be worthwhile.
- Supporting the people around us - making sure that our family or our employees are well cared for and prosper.
- Doing what we consider to be the 'right' thing - it is my duty as his daughter to visit him once a week, even if he no longer recognises me.
- Improving ourselves - activities that will help us to be the kind of people that we want to be.

In all of these, the meaning comes from having a sense of greater purpose. When we generate that sense of purpose ourselves it is more likely to contribute to our happiness than if we simply adopt one that somebody else - society, parents or employers - impose on us. The boy who suffers a childhood injustice and, as a result, becomes a lawyer devoted to making the world a fairer place, is likely to have a richer and happier work experience than his colleague whose sees himself as simply working for an income, or to achieve social status.

Equally, the committed environmentalist derives greater happiness when she takes her bottles to be recycled than her neighbour, who does so simply because her friends do.

If we are to spend our time in a way that will make us happy, we need to have an idea of what we're aiming towards. Identifying these three sources is a useful start, and keeping them in mind will certainly help us to make informed decisions about what will give us satisfaction. The picture becomes much richer, however, when we combine them.

A picture of happiness

When we combine the three sources we get a picture of what makes us happy that looks like this:

Happiness multibuy

There are, of course, many things that won't fit on this diagram because they don't contribute to our happiness. But if they do, they will have a place on here somewhere.

Our goal, therefore, is to spend the majority of our time doing things that fit on this picture, ideally in the overlapping segments or, best of all, in the centre. First, though, it helps to be clear about what each section means and to identify where those things that we already do fit on the diagram.

Hedonism - pure pleasure

This is where many start their search for happiness, and quite a few end it.

However, even hedonism isn't straightforward. One of the difficulties we have when we pursue pure pleasure is spotting the difference between what we crave and what we enjoy. Satisfying a craving may bring short term pleasure, like the relief of scratching an itch, but it soon fades. And then a bigger craving takes its place, then another and another and so on. This is known as the 'hedonistic treadmill', and it can be an exhausting and frustrating place to be.

I may think a new car will make me happy but, when I get one, it doesn't seem to hit the spot and soon I find myself craving a bigger car, then a second car, then a four-wheel drive, and so on. The question is, what's the itch that I am trying to scratch?

It often has little to do with the actual thing that we are craving and a lot more to do with comparing ourselves with others or reinforcing our identity. Advertisers do a great job of keeping the hedonistic treadmill turning, presenting a car as an intrinsic part of boardroom power and sexual success rather than simply, well, a car. As a result of these kinds of message we are seduced into believing that acquisition is the route to pleasure. It's an understandable mistake in a society that is constantly encouraging us to spend money - but it's a costly one when it comes to having a good time.

Our first challenge is to identify the difference between those things that we want simply to satisfy a craving and those things that will actually give us a lasting, satisfying pleasure: a sunset, stimulating friends, a log fire, or even a car that's a pleasure to drive.

The second is to be aware that when we are on the 'hedonistic treadmill', good experiences fade fast. More of the same won't be enough any longer. We will find ourselves craving more and more possessions and luxuries just to maintain our current level of pleasure.

The third is to realise that pleasure isn't the whole game.

Why we're hooked on hedonism

Some social commentators argue that in previous eras strengths such as fortitude and resilience were more highly regarded. By contrast, in today's consumerist society, they argue, we see instant gratification almost as our right. As a result, the 'me' generation of today is much more inclined to give up at the first sign of difficulty and go elsewhere for immediate pleasure rather than persist and enjoy the deeper sense of happiness that comes with challenge and overcoming the odds.

Whether this is correct or not, we are all still rational people. So why, even when we know that achieving a challenge will make us happier, do we still opt for the lesser 'pleasure'? Why, when we know that reading a book or going for a run will do more for us than watching TV or raiding the fridge, do we so often find ourselves slumped on the sofa with a slice of cold pizza?

There are six primary reasons. Not all of them apply in every situation but usually more than one is at play when we settle for the instant hedonistic hit over the more deeply enjoyable challenge.

- Possible failure - if I don't achieve the challenge I might end up less happy than not trying in the first place.
- Skill, effort and discipline - it requires more exertion, sometimes considerably more. I feel like a rest, at least right now.
- It will produce a change - the result will be a situation that is different from what I've got now. It can feel more comfortable to stick with what we know than risk the uncertain.
- Constraint - once I commit to this challenge I am likely to reduce my room for manoeuvre; if a new opportunity crops up I won't be able to take it without leaving this challenge half done.
- Anxiety - I'm worried about what might happen; this isn't a pleasant feeling so I choose a more instantly comfortable route.
- Opportunity cost - maybe I could be doing something that would make me happier instead.

So, what's getting in the way of your happy day?

Rapture - pleasure/challenge

When an activity stretches us at the same time as giving us pleasure, we are experiencing rapture. Doing a triathlon, playing the piano, making hollandaise sauce - anything that we enjoy doing and which also uses our skills, is likely to be in this section, combining pleasure and challenge.

When we lose ourselves in a game of tennis, when we're absorbed in solving a crossword, cracking through a report or fiercely debating the merits of one pro golfer over another, we can lose track of how we feel. If we were interrupted and asked if we were enjoying ourselves, we would say yes. Pleasure is present throughout this activity, although we might be so engrossed that we don't realise it until afterwards.

This is in contrast with our experience in 'captivated' mode (see below) where we will not be experiencing direct pleasure whilst we're doing the activity although we will feel happy afterwards.

Captivated - pure challenge

No pain, no gain.

Some tasks require significant effort and don't provide us with much pleasure whilst we are doing them. So why would we include them on our happiness diagram? It could be fixing the car, the dog's

injections or the kids' clothes for the school play. However, afterwards we are likely to feel the rich satisfaction that comes from a difficult job well done.

Things are tricky at work. Your pet project is in danger of being lost as everyone suddenly seems to be finding fault and the willing consensus that you thought you'd gathered appears to have evaporated. You feel like giving up. But you don't. Instead, you swallow your anger, navigate the politics, fight the battles you need to and accommodate where it is possible. It is a painful process but, meeting after tricky meeting, sensitive email after back covering voicemail, pride swallowing diplomacy after fulsome flattery, you slowly win your colleagues round. And, finally, your project gets the go-ahead, you feel a great sense of achievement. The journey may not have been enjoyable but the outcome definitely makes you feel elated.

This is the kind of triumph that makes us happy. It doesn't need to be at work. It could just as well be finishing the shelves in the hall or finally clearing out the cupboard under the stairs. The key is that though the experience itself wasn't especially enjoyable, the result was more than worth the pain to get there.

Good works - challenge/meaning

 There are some difficult things that we do because they need to be done - whether to help others or to help ourselves further down the line.

Standing in a rainy street with a charity box trying to encourage hurried shoppers to donate; going to night school to get a degree; getting fit; giving up smoking - all of these require effort and hardship. They also all contribute to something more than the outcome itself: fresh water in the Third World; a new career; a healthy life.

Good works aren't the first place most people look for happiness. Nonetheless, people who are in this zone tend to be happier than those with the hedonistic lifestyle, even if they don't know it.

You're happy but do you know it?

Mihaly Csikszentmihalyi asked two groups of school children to report on how they spent their time and how they felt whilst they were doing it. He found that those who had hobbies, played sports and worked on their homework, scored higher on almost all measures of psychological wellbeing than the teenagers who spent their time hanging around in shopping malls. They also went on to higher education, had better social lives and were more successful in later life.

Interestingly, even though this group performed so well against the psychological measures, when the experimenters asked them who they thought were having the better time, they said that the teenagers down the mall were having more fun and they would like to join them.

The lure of pleasure can overshadow the other sources of happiness. Which only goes to show, not only can happiness be found in unexpected places, but also we may not recognise it when we've got it.

Duty - pure meaning

Stuffing envelopes for a charity; visiting a sick rela-
tive; clearing waste land to make a children's
playground - none of these necessarily require much
skill and they might not provide high levels of sensory pleasure, but they may contribute a great deal
to our wellbeing. If we believe that we are doing something
good or worthwhile, that fact alone can make us feel happier.

Of course, it's not always easy to keep sight of the mission when the
task is truly disagreeable. Changing the nappies of our six-month-
old daughter is not exactly difficult and it's not particularly pleasant.
However, when we remind ourselves of the purpose, that we are
making our much loved daughter healthy and comfortable, then
even a task as unappealing as nappy changing can help us be
happy.

Between a rock and a hard place

Duties can also be a source of tension. If we do what we want to do
- spend the weekend away - we will feel guilty. But if we do what we
know we should do - have our parents to stay - we are likely to feel
resentful. Overcoming this is not always easy, but realising that both
choices can add to our happiness can help. Once we have made the
choice, we need to make an effort to experience the kind of satisfaction that is on offer: pleasure or duty. Then we will find it is easier
to let go of our worries about the other option and will be free to
enjoy what we are doing with our time.

And, if we can find a way to make the duty pleasurable as well as
meaningful, then so much the better.

Meaning matters

People who see their work as a 'calling' not only enjoy it much
more but also consider their lives happier and their health
better than those who describe their work as a job or a career.

In an extensive study, psychologists asked a group of people
in a range of occupations how they thought about their work.

Job: I do this primarily for the material gain so that I can enjoy
the rest of my life.

Career: I do this because I believe it will help me progress into future, better roles.

Calling: I do this because I love it and I believe that it helps make the world a better place.

The descriptions in the original experiment were longer but the gist was much the same. Each person allocated points across the three descriptions depending on how much they felt they applied to their work. In the sample, there was an even spread across all three, even within groups who were doing the same role.

As well as being happier and healthier, those who described their work according to the definition of a 'calling', were significantly more likely to talk about what they did outside work and encourage other people to take up the same line of work. They were also much less likely to say, 'Thank God it's Friday!'

Welcome responsibilities - pleasure/meaning

Here we are doing something that makes a difference beyond the act itself - and we are enjoying the act of doing it.

Maybe our bed-ridden uncle is a wise old bird with a store of scurrilous stories, or we're thoroughly enjoying the book we have to read for the exam, or the networking evening has turned out to be full of interesting people.

It's what you might call a win-win situation: doing something that we ought to do and loving every minute of it. No pain, much gain.

For one workout participant, however, this kind of situation had a nasty way of becoming a win-lose. She felt that, when a duty became pleasurable, it was somehow less of a duty. Like delicious cough mixture that tastes too good to be medicine, she believed that unless the duty was unpleasant it didn't count. Lurking behind this assumption was the belief that duty must be selfless and if she was enjoying it, how can it be selfless?

Understandable, but unhelpful. Looking for the pleasure in duties is one sure route to a happier life.

Joy - pleasure/challenge/meaning

This is where we are likely to find the greatest and most enduring happiness, when all three elements come together.

It can be very significant occasions - the final; the first night; the pitch; when you propose; when you accept. But it doesn't have to be. Pleasure, challenge and meaning can come together in all sorts of small and unexpected moments.

Veterans of World War II often talk about their war years being the happiest years of their life. For those who've never been close to armed conflict this might seem odd - how could the ravages of battle possibly be a source of happiness? However, all three sources of wellbeing are likely to have been in full display.

The meaning came from a patriotic duty to fight for their country and what they believed was right. The challenge from the extremely difficult and often life threatening conditions. And the pleasure from the camaraderie with the people around them, which was often intensified by the extreme threats they were facing.

Fortunately, we don't have to have been in a battle to recognise that the happiest lives belong to those who spend most of their time where these three sources of happiness meet.

Make me happy

Using the picture of happiness there are three ways we can increase the amount of time when we are feeling good:

1　Change the way we think about or do those activities that we don't much enjoy

2　Set ourselves up so that what we do is more likely to be in the happiness picture

3　Move around the picture to areas where the circles overlap so that what we do gives greater joy

1　Get in the picture

I have to do the weekly supermarket visit and it doesn't make me happy. What can I do?

Assuming you can't persuade someone else to do it or order online, here are some of the ways you could try to get the weekly trek round the ailes into the happiness picture:

Pleasure
- Go somewhere where you can taste new delicacies
- Choose a shop where the staff know you and are friendly
- Go with a friend

Challenge
- Try to beat your personal best for how long it takes to complete the full shop
- Go somewhere new
- Buy at least two things you've never cooked (or heard of) before

Meaning
- Consider it as part of your role in creating a happy household
- Choose local shops and see this as a way of helping local business people
- Shop organic and feel that you're doing your bit for the environment, and your health

Even with the most mundane tasks we have the opportunity to make them a source of some happiness, which means that we're going to feel better about our time spent doing them.

2 Write me a mission

When we have our own mission or sense of purpose it's much easier to choose to do things that are going to contribute to our happiness.

One technique popular with life coaches is to encourage their clients to write the obituary they would like. The coach and client then look for common themes and use these to craft a description of purpose or personal mission. Once they've agreed on this, the next step is to search for ways to achieve it (of which more in chapter H, Pathfinder).

Another approach is to reflect on the impact of what we do and use this to identify our purpose. For example, the guide who shows tourists round their town may deduce that their mission, at least at work, is to make holidays happy, to educate people, to enhance the reputation of the town or to improve the local economy. Once he's decided on his purpose it will be much easier to get involved in other things that will support this mission. He might previously have regarded organising the town fête, helping out in the youth club or running for election as a councillor as a burden. But if they are part of achieving his more encompassing goal then they will have meaning and so are much more likely to feel like time well spent.

3 Getting to joy

Once we're in the happiness picture, we're already in a good place. However, it doesn't mean we can't make it better.

Duty, captivated, hedonism; all these are great states to be in. But they represent only one of the three sources of wellbeing. We are likely to be even happier when we are drawing from more than one source.

We have seen how making duties pleasurable, or adding an element of challenge, can enrich the experience and lead us to feel that our time is well spent. The same applies to activities that sit in the Captivated and Hedonist sections. Being captivated is even better if what captivates us also helps achieve our purpose and gives us pleasure.

Each situation will be different and we will need to develop our own way of adding in additional sources of happiness. Here are a few general suggestions:

Add pleasure

- Make it funny - any job is better when we get to laugh too.

- Include treats along the way.

- Do the activity somewhere stimulating or unusual.

- Bring along other sympathetic people.

Add challenge
- Try to find a way of achieving the same outcome using a different method.

- Add some extra outcomes that you want to achieve as well.

- Raise the standards for what you consider acceptable, or excellent.

- Try to do it in less time.

Add meaning

- Consider what good things this says about you - how does it reinforce or enhance your identity as a kind/romantic/creative/courageous person?

- What's the impact? And the benefit? Keep asking these questions until you can link what you're doing to a cause you care about.

- Think about what you will be able to do as a result of completing this activity that you couldn't have done before.

- Reflect on how you will be better off intellectually, physically, emotionally or even financially as a result of what you are doing.

Happy thoughts

Once we know how to be happy we are well on the way to knowing how to spend our time wisely. As Abraham Lincoln observed, 'Most folk are as happy as they make up their minds to be.'

(H) Pathfinder

Ever considered choosing what to do on the roll of a dice?

If I roll a one I'll paint the bathroom, a two I'll break into the flat downstairs, a three and I'll make a sandwich, a four and I'll cycle around the square naked, a five and I'll go to bed until tomorrow morning and a six I will spend the next week speaking in rhyming couplets.

The protagonist in Luke Reinhardt's novel, *The Diceman*, uses a technique like this. It's certainly a novel approach if a bit risky, particularly if you keep throwing a four - nude cycling could lose its appeal when winter sets in.

Many of us have equally quirky ways of engaging with destiny. Some people read their horoscope, others spin pendulums or consult fortune cookies; one workout participant pulls fridge magnets out of a bag to get guidance. Like the dice roll, these methods may be unscientific but they all represent a desire to make a decision, to choose a path - even if it is one decided by a fortune cookie.

Clarity about where we're heading gives us more control and means we make better decisions about how we use our time. Should we go into business on our own or cut back on our work responsibilities and spend more time with our children? Should we follow our lover when they move to a new country or stay put and stick with our plan to study? If we can clarify what we want and set a direction for ourselves, we are much more likely to make a good call on how we use our time - after all, it's helping us achieve something that we know we want.

The path we choose won't be set in stone - life will continue to pitch us enough curved balls to provide variety - it simply means we're stacking the odds in our favour. Think of it as a satellite navigation system for your life, reminding you where you are, suggesting short-cuts, dealing with diversions, but always keeping the final destination in mind - unless you choose to change it, of course.

Just imagine …

If you've ever done creative writing lessons at school or since you've probably been asked to dream up a character and then describe a period in their future. For example, you might have been asked to list all the events that are going to take place in their family life in the next year. From this material you fill out their story, you decide what choices they will have to make and why, to lead them along that par-ticular path. For many writers this is a wonderfully liberating exercise - a chance to play God, as Martin Amis describes it.

In this direction-setting exercise we are going to do something simi-lar, except here you are the character whose future life is being described. But there's still room to stretch your imagination. If you don't like the plan you come up with you can edit and adapt it as many times as you like. And nobody needs to see it if you don't want them to. So don't hold back.

To make things simple we are going to consider our future direction in seven life areas.

- Physical - how we look and feel

- Mental - our learning, skills and our state of mind

- Social - our relationships with friends

- Occupational - our work

- Financial - how we handle money matters

- Familial - our relationship with our family

- Intimate - our intimate relationships

We're now going to go through an exercise to think about the year ahead. There are three steps:

Step one - Answer the questions below. You don't have to answer them immediately. You don't even have to answer all of them. You may want to reflect and mull over some of the answers before you commit them to paper.

Step two - Look through your answers and highlight the ones you'd most like to focus on. It's unlikely that you'll be able to achieve everything so this is where you examine priorities and start making choices.

Step three - Ask whether you are willing to invest the time and make the requisite changes to achieve the goals you've identified.

Step one - Explore

Get relaxed and give yourself some space. This may not be the best thing to reflect on if you're in a stuffy train. Once you're comfortable take a moment to think about the life you'd like to be living in a year's time. Don't worry about whether you think it's possible, just focus on what the ideal would be.

So, imagine yourself in a year, just 12 months from now, then read on.

Physical

How do you feel?

How do you look?

How fit are you?

How do others describe you in terms of physical appearance?

How much do you exercise?

What type of exercise?

What are you eating?

What are you drinking?

How much are you smoking?

Are there any health issues that you have been putting off that are now resolved?

Mental

How are you using your mind/talents in a way that makes you feel fulfilled?

What new skills/knowledge have you acquired?

What books, newspapers, journals are you reading?

What other learning experiences have you had?

What are you an expert in?

What do others say about your expertise? How would they describe you in terms of your state of mind?

What mental capabilities are you most proud of?

Is there someone who inspires you who you are able to spend more time with?

Have you overcome any personal barriers to using your mind?

Social

What's your social life like?

How are you using your social time?

Who are you spending more time with?

Who are you spending less time with?

Have you expanded/reduced your circle of friends?

What clubs have you joined?

How often have you got out?

What social skills have you developed?

What are you like to be around socially?

How would your friends describe you?

What do your friends most appreciate about you?

What do you give your friends?

Occupational

What are you doing work-wise?

How fulfilled are you?

Are you using your talents/skills to their maximum? How?

What have you achieved?

How are you managing your career?

What are you like to work with?

What are you like to work for?

What relationships do you have with your work colleagues?

What work habits have changed?

Is there an outstanding work issue that you've now dealt with? If so, what?

What does your work environment look and feel like?

Financial

What is your financial situation?

How much are you earning?

How much are your debts?

How much are your savings and investments?

What are your significant assets (eg, house, car)?

How important is money to you?

How much money is enough?

What money related habits have you changed?

How are you spending money differently?

What are you most proud to say you have achieved financially?

Familial

What are you like as a family member?

As a parent?

Brother/sister?

Daughter/son?

What is important about family for you?

How is your relationship different now to the way it was a year ago?

What would your family say about their relationship with you?

Are there any family issues which have been resolved (eg, spending more time together, mending a split)?

How do you represent your family to others?

Intimate/Sentimental

What relationship, if any, are you in?

What does the other person think of you?

What are you feelings for the other person?

How do people outside your closest relationship see it?

What boundaries are there in the relationship?

What are you getting from the other person?

What are you giving to the other person?

Step two - Focus

Having gone through your answers, choose the five events, activities or areas that seem most interesting or important for you to focus on in the coming year. List them below.

1.

2.

3.

4.

5.

One participant who attended The Mind Gym workout on this subject reported back a couple of months later. 'I feel much happier now. I have finally got fit and I've started to sing again, which is something I've wanted to do for a long time.' She felt that her time was, at last, well spent.

OK, so that gives us some focus, but is it a balanced view?

Tough choices

We often want to do more than there is time for. If you're looking at the answers to your questions and wondering how you'll manage to do everything on the list, the answer is fairly simple. You probably won't. If you are dissatisfied with that answer, or frustrated that you have to make a choice, turn to chapter A, Hawks and doves. If, however, you're not sure what the right choice is, think about the three routes to happiness in chapter G - Joy division. Ask yourself which of your options will give you the greatest amount of pleasure, challenge and meaning.

Step three - Deliver

Finally we consider whether we believe that these activities are worth using our time to achieve.

If you feel you now have enough to go on and that your destination is clear, you've done enough. If not, the next chapter on goal setting will help you turn a low fidelity general direction into a high fidelity precision target.

Making it happen

So we've now got an idea of what we want the year ahead to look like. But what does that mean in practice? Will we, in truth, have time to give to the activities that we have identified as important? Or will the 'stuff of life' take over? To answer that question, and to set about making the time available, we need to take a look at our daily life and ask ourselves:

Where does the time go?

From a roll of the dice to a role in life

As individuals we take on many roles - parent, friend, mentor, cook, cleaner, phone answering service, etc. - and all these roles take up time. Sometimes they get out of balance and one role dominates our time to the detriment of the others. This can easily happen without our noticing it, so a regular check-up on how much time we are spending on each of our roles can be very useful.

Maggie, a workout participant, described her primary roles as insurance broker, mother, partner, chauffeur, chef, cleaner, friend, daughter, domestic goddess and painter. Her dream was to do more painting but she found that, with her busy career and home life, the thing that made her most engaged was relegated to a very part-time hobby. She completed the chart below, allocating how much of her total time she spent in each role.

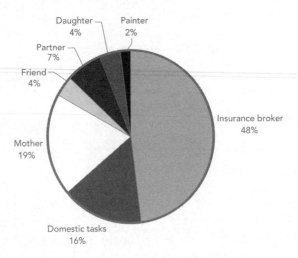

Maggie had already highlighted that her role as painter needed more time. Now she faced the question of which activities she would do less of to gain that time. Having completed the chart above it became clear that her role of domestic goddess was taking up far more time than she thought. Reluctant to reduce any of the other areas, she decided it was her inner Nigella that would have to go.

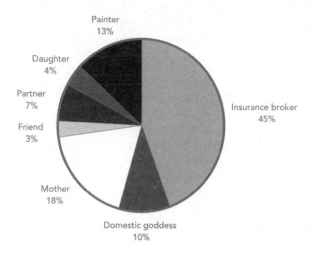

Having decided what she wanted to focus on, Maggie believed she would now feel better about how she spent her time. But she was also aware of the downsides. There would be fewer homemade meals, she would have to persuade her partner to do more of the domestic chores and there wouldn't be time for quite as many after work drinks.

Over to you

If you have come to some decisions about the direction you want to take in the next year, the next step is to consider what impact that will have on your many and varied life roles.

First think about the roles that you play in your life and write them in the space below. Consider every activity and what roles they give you. At this point, don't worry about grouping roles, just get everything down.

Now it's time to amalgamate. Are some roles essentially the same? (For example friend, host and free counsellor.) It's best if you have six or seven major roles rather than twenty-five little activities.

1   5

2   6

3   7

4

Think about the average number of hours you spend on each of these activities per week and complete the pie chart below. We've put markers in for every 10% or the rough equivalent of 10 waking hours. (If you're sleeping roughly 8 hours a night with a bit of a lie-in on the weekend, then a percentage point is broadly equal to an hour's activity.)

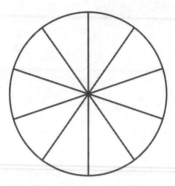

Now consider, given the answers you gave to the questions above, what you would like your ideal pie chart to look like. You may also want to introduce new roles at this point depending on your earlier answers.

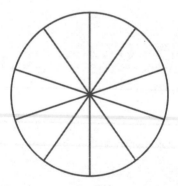

Your role

At this point, you will have some ideas about what this year's direction should be and what impact that will have on your various roles. The next couple of chapters will give you an idea of how to set goals within these roles, how to get the best return on your time, and how to plan and prioritise to ensure you meet your goals.

(I) Goal getting

A group of workout participants were asked to think about an occasion when they felt really satisfied with their use of time. Be specific, they were told - remember an episode when things were exactly as you wanted them to be, when you felt they couldn't have been any better. A good time, a happy time, time well spent.

The group came up with a dizzying array of examples: an early morning run, a speech at a conference, playing the piano, an hour spent learning to dance, a pottery class, singing in a choir, chairing a meeting, a dinghy race, the London to Brighton bike ride, writing a love letter, a juggling lesson.

The participants were then asked to recall that experience in as much detail as possible and to describe how they were feeling at the time.

'I was in the zone'
'In the groove'
'Everything just clicked'
'I felt I had hit my stride'
'As though nothing could go wrong'

Interestingly these feel-good experiences weren't always to do with success. The sailor hadn't won the dinghy race and the pianist didn't manage a note-perfect rendition of a Chopin nocturne. It was something else that had made these moments so satisfying, something in the quality of the experience, something that psychologists call Flow.

Let the good times flow

The psychologist Mihaly Csikszentmihalyi set out to discover what was happening when people described themselves as being 'in the groove'. He gave a group of people beepers that went off at random times of day and asked them to write down what they were doing and how they felt at the moment the bleeper went off. Having collected a vast amount of data he found that whether he was studying a Japanese motorcycle gang or Bulgarian chess players the conditions and the resulting feelings were the same. People felt most satisfied and described themselves as happiest when they were thoroughly engaged and engrossed with an experience. Csikszentmihalyi described this as having an 'autotelic' experience and named the resulting state as 'Flow'.

Flow experiences are absorbing, engrossing, sometimes even enlightening. More surprising, when it comes to time well spent, they tend to score higher than the sedentary states that we normally associate with happiness, like lying in a hammock on a sunny day. It's not that blissful relaxation is a poor use of time, far from it, it can be essential and extremely rewarding, only that being immersed in a challenge is, overall, more likely to make us happy and believe that our time is well spent.

Flow experiences are good. However, in many people's minds they are also a consequence of good luck. Asked to explain the cause of their flow moments most of the workout participants described them as a fluke or simply inexplicable - 'I must have got out of the right side of the bed.' 'It just happened.' 'I have no idea how I got there.'

But that's not the case. In fact, getting into flow is something that we can do consciously and deliberately. It is under our control. To find out how to get into flow, and stay there, read on.

Results guaranteed

Goals work, there is little doubt about it. Edwin Locke, one of the first psychologists to study this area, suggests that setting a goal will increase performance by 16%. In terms of time, that's an hour saved over an eight hour working day. More evidence comes from a study that measured college students' attitudes towards time and compared them with each student's grade scores over the course of a four-year degree. It turned out that those students who set themselves goals felt they had greater control over their time and they also achieved a significantly higher overall grade average.

In another study truck drivers increased the logs loaded on their trucks from 60% to 90% of their legal allowable weight as a result of assigned goals. The drivers saved the company $250,000 in 9 months.

And goals work their magic with all ages. A group of young children were asked to jump over a bar. The control group managed to jump the bar an average of 3.8 times but the children with specific goals jumped the bar 6.9 times.

Who's goal is it anyway?

Can we set goals for others, or should we always agree them collaboratively? The research suggests that as long as a goal is communicated with logic and a compelling rationale both approaches are equally motivating. However, from a problem solving perspective, there are great benefits to including an individual in goal setting as they are then already thinking through what could be done to make the goal happen.

So the evidence is strong but the practice, it seems, is weak. Looking at Harvard Business School students, researchers discovered that only 3% set clear written goals. Ten years later those 3% were earning ten times the other 97% combined. Of course, this may have been due to many other factors such as drive, commitment and conscientiousness, but it would be churlish to dismiss goals as playing no part.

Own goal

So, why don't more of us set goals? Possibly because we have tried in the past and it hasn't worked.

Blame it on the New Year. All those big, highfalutin resolutions that we make: 'lose weight', 'get fit', 'learn Spanish'. Then, when after three months we still can't do anything more than order a beer in the local tapas bar, we give in and declare the enterprise a failure. The problem is that the goals we set ourselves are often just too big or too generalised and so, as a result, even when we attempt to achieve them, we don't perform at our best. (In fact, the research shows that we perform better with no goal at all, rather than with a goal that we feel is beyond our reach.)

When it comes to setting useful, motivating goals, the one-size-fits-all approach rarely works. Instead we need to custom build them. The key is getting the right balance between the challenge we set ourselves and the skills we have to achieve it - and that will be different for each one of us.

It takes a bit of thought, but if you want to order some food to go with that bottle of cerveza, it's well worth it.

How can I tell if my goal is in balance?

Think of a goal that you would like to achieve. Now think of the activity that this goal involves and ask yourself, honestly, what level of skill you have in that activity. Taking our example of learning Spanish, if you've never spoken a word in your life, never attended a class and aren't entirely sure where Spain is on the map, you should be describing yourself as low skill.

But if your partner is Spanish and you visit Seville regularly, you're likely to have a head start, at least you know what the language sounds like. You have some skill but not a lot. If, however, you've studied Spanish to degree level, then taught in Madrid for a year, your skill level is likely to be quite considerable and you might describe yourself as highly skilled.

Once you have an idea of the amount of skill you are starting with, you can decide what level of challenge you need to give yourself a great chance of performing at your best and experiencing that fabulous flow buzz.

When balancing skill with challenge, there are four potential outcomes.

Slack

This is the lowest level of challenge, when you could do the task in your sleep. Our degree level speaker attending a 'First steps in Spanish' course would be in slack. She might enjoy the company, she might even get some pleasure out of being the smartest person in the class, but the lesson will have nothing to offer her; she will quickly become bored and unfulfilled and a million miles from flow.

Straightforward

The student with a little less knowledge, regular holidays in Andalusia and a Spanish exchange in Cadiz but no formal qualifications, would have a different experience at the same class. He wouldn't be bored exactly, but he wouldn't be stimulated. He'd be coasting. For him, this would be a straightforward goal and, as a result, not particularly engaging.

Stretch

Our complete beginner, however, stands a very good chance of experiencing the joys of flow in this class. As she has no prior knowledge of the language she is outside her comfort zone - but not too far as this is an introductory class. She is being stretched and may well end the class feeling motivated and fulfilled.

Strain

If, however, our beginner has reading difficulties or doesn't speak the same language as the teacher or any of the other students, she will probably experience strain.

Without stabilisers - stretch or strain?

To keep ourselves flowing we need a goal that stretches without strain.

Where do we stretch?

In the work/home balance, where do we find most flow?

To find out, a group of researchers gave a wide selection of people pagers that beeped randomly eight times over the course of the day. When the pager beeped, the participants wrote down what they were doing, the level of challenge of the activity and the amount of skill required. They also reported on how they were feeling.

Given that flow makes us happy, we might expect to find a greater amount of flow in our leisure time. However, people reported being in flow on 54% of occasions whilst at work, but only 18% the rest of the time.

We don't always get it right, of course. Sometimes we over-estimate our skill and feel overwhelmed; other times we aim too low and end up bored or drifting. But if we're aware of the idea of flow we're more likely to recognise our difficulty as an out of balance goal, rather than a personal failure.

Setting a flow-friendly goal

Jo is planning to run the New York marathon. She wants to set herself some goals: for the number of hours it will take her to run 26 miles, and the amount of money she will raise for charity. She did London in 4½ hours and raised £350.

Jo's options for the goals she could set herself look something like this:

	Slack	Straightforward	Stretch	Strain
Marathon run time	5 hrs	4½ hrs	4 hrs	3½ hrs
Amount raised for charity	£100	£350	£700	£1,000

To perform at her best she decides that a goal of four hours is the one to go for and a target sponsorship of £700. If she doesn't consider this to be enough she could perhaps ask her sponsors for a higher rate per mile, rather than pushing herself to run faster. Aiming to complete the course in 3½ hours would move her into a strain goal, which will likely reduce her performance and mean that she'll enjoy the experience much less.

The same approach can be applied to more complex ambitions. Say we want to improve our presentation skills. There are a number of factors that could affect the level of challenge involved. How long are we speaking for and to how many people? With notes, cue cards, or off the cuff? How much do we know about the subject already? Some of these elements may be out of our control - the size of the audience for example. But it is probably down to us whether we use notes or not, and how well prepared we are. So we do have some room for manoeuvre when we're setting the level of challenge.

Skills in public speaking vary enormously and the following grid may not reflect your own experience, but it will give you an idea of what a goal setting grid might look like.

	Slack	Straightforward	Stretch	Strain
Length of time	1 min	5 min	20 min	An hour
Familiarity of topic	Very familiar	Familiar	New	Unknown
Notes	Speech to read out	Lots of cue cards	A single cue card	Nothing
Size of audience	3	8	20	60
Makeup of audience	People who work for me	My peers	More senior people	Strangers

The stretch goal for this person is 20 minutes talking on a new topic to 20 more senior people with a single cue card. They may find that idea daunting but then that's how it should be. If a goal doesn't generate a 'yikes' in your stomach then it probably isn't a stretch goal. It is meant to be a challenge, after all.

This is how we can get into flow and so into a state where we are likely to think that our time is well spent. But just because we've got there doesn't mean we'll stay there.

A step up

If we suspect our goal may be a strain it doesn't mean that we have to dilute it. We can increase our skills for a start. And there are other ways to increase our motivation and so get the goal within our stretch.

1 Supersize

If your goal provides multiple benefits it will feel an even better use of your time. So, don't just aim to cycle to Istanbul - get a company to sponsor you and pitch the story to a travel magazine.

2 Share

Other people can be great motivators. The more of them you get onside, the more likely you are to keep at it. And if you come across someone who doesn't think you can make it - use that as a spur to prove them wrong.

3 Up close and personal

Make the benefits tangible and specific. It's not just a promotion but the salary increase that will mean you can get a new house, a new car, or a new nose.

4 Big Picture

Think through the ramifications, good as well as bad, and it will be easier to deal with whatever comes along the way.

Staying in flow

'Too much of a good thing can be wonderful.' Mae West

Stretch goals are a powerful tool to get us into a state of flow. They aren't, however, always enough to keep us there. Here are some tactics that can help.

One step at a time

Think small

Break the big task into smaller, easily achievable steps and focus on these one at a time. Tell yourself you're aiming to make it to the next bend in the road and forget about the twenty more to come. As the legendary Chinese proverb states, 'A journey of a thousand miles starts with a single step.'

Work with what you've got

If the environment isn't ideal and you can't change it, don't let it distract you. Tell yourself that things are the best that they can possibly be at the moment and then move your attention to your task in hand.

Live for the moment

The past is a different country and the future is one you haven't visited yet. Stick with the present - that's where flow happens. Try as hard as you can to silence the 'what ifs' and the 'if onlys'. Concentrate on the detail in the current moment - the tap of the keys, the feel of the ground under your feet, the weight of the paintbrush.

Assess the impact

Be on the lookout for feedback (which is not necessarily the same as praise). Notice the impact of your actions at every level and you will be able to make the small adjustments necessary to stay in flow.

Parkinson plus

Two psychologists, Joseph McGrath and Janice Kelly, set out to test Parkinson's law: 'work expands to fill the time available for its completion'.

A series of small groups of people were given tasks to do which involved working out five-letter anagrams. They did these in three different lengths of time: 5 minutes, 10 minutes and 20 minutes. Those who started with the shorter 5-minute interval would then do the 10-minute and finally the 20-minute interval. And those who started with the 20-minute interval would then go to 10 minutes and then 5 minutes. On some occasions the workload, in terms of the number of anagrams to be solved, was varied according to the length of time.

The experiment proved Parkinson's law: the more anagrams a group was asked to solve the more it solved, and the fewer a group was given, the fewer it did.

More surprisingly, it also revealed that performance was affected by the sequence in which the subjects experienced the time intervals. The people who started with the shorter, more demanding 5-minute time intervals and progressed to the longer ones, performed faster in all time intervals than the people who started with the longer 20-minute interval and progressed to the shorter one.

This research suggests that our first experience sets our pace. A stretch at the outset improves our performance even when the challenge becomes less demanding later. And if we start with the easy option we will find it more difficult to rise to the bigger challenges.

Let yourself be

Once in flow it can be tempting to step back and admire our performance - rather like the small child in the school play who can't resist coming to the front of the stage to wave at mum and dad. Try to avoid interrupting yourself, respect the process and allow yourself to stay engrossed.

Enjoy it

Remember flow contributes to happiness and happiness = a sense of time well spent. So forget the tough moments and concentrate on the joyful parts of the experience.

I TRY Give my mind a workout

Have a go at setting stretch goals for something you want or need to do. If the objective doesn't have an in-built deadline you might choose to make this one of the factors.

Activity / objective:

Effort / Factors	Slack	Straight-forward	Stretch	Strain

(J) Planning for non-planners

'Would you tell me, please, which way I ought to go from here?'
said Alice.

'That depends a good deal on where you want to get to,' said the
Cat.

'I don't care much where,' said Alice.

'Then is doesn't matter which way you go,' said the Cat.

Alice in Wonderland by Lewis Carroll

Most of us want to get somewhere. And usually we want to get there as quickly and efficiently as possible. To achieve this, a plan of some kind may seem an essential bit of kit, the obvious first step, a no-brainer, in fact. But is it? Some people find creating plans a real chore, whilst others never get beyond them, spending more time cross-referencing the dependencies and highlighting the contingencies than actually doing any of the tasks that will help them on their way.

So, are plans worth the effort and, if so, how much? And, for those of us who find the whole business of creating a detailed route map as miserable as a Monday morning, how can we make planning pleasurable as well as useful?

Because it's worth it

Planning certainly improves performance if you are a business. Studies that have measured the impact of planning on performance and profitability have found that, yes, there is a clear link. One survey examined fifty start-up businesses, half of which had a business plan before they started trading and half of which did not.

Those with a business plan markedly outperformed those which didn't have one, whether the business plan was followed or not.

The group that plans together works together. Numerous experiments have shown that working collaboratively to plot a path helps all those involved build stronger relationships and generate a deeper, shared understanding about what needs to be done. This allows individuals to make good decisions (at least ones that the rest of the group will support) by themselves at a later stage. The time investment up front can deliver a great return when unexpected things happen later on.

The research about planning for ourselves is more equivocal. The good news is that a little appears to go a long way. Research suggests that we get the optimal return when we spend no more than 1% of the time the task will take on planning. An hour per day, they argue, can be saved with 10 minutes of smart preparation.

But there is a downside. Planning can be a form of procrastination. A revision timetable before exams helps us understand the size of the task ahead, but it becomes a major hindrance if we then spend our entire time colour coding, amending and updating rather than doing the actual revising. Too much time spent planning can seduce us into thinking that we are getting a lot done, whereas in fact we haven't even made a start.

On balance, planning is a good thing provided we don't go too detailed or let it take up too much of our time. Napoleon probably got it right when he said: '*I have always found that plans are useless but the act of planning is indispensable.*'

It'll only take two ticks

When Samuel Johnson began compiling the first dictionary in 1857 he believed that it would take him two years. As it turned out Johnson's estimate was a little out - the first edition was published seventy years after he started.

Underestimating happens to all of us. We may not be as wide of the mark as Johnson but we do repeatedly assume that things will take less time than they do - even when previous attempts provide evidence to the contrary. This over-optimism has a technical name: the planning fallacy. Interestingly, it appears that the fallacy applies when we estimate how long a project will take when we are going to do it ourselves. However, if we're not responsible for the outcome then our prediction is far more accurate.

When researchers asked people to estimate the amount of time someone else's challenge would take to complete, they found little error. When we look at other people's projects we take into account previous experiences and deadlines, but when we consider our own projects we tend to ignore the evidence and assume that everything will run smoothly this time.

Worse still is if we're in a team who are all going to be involved in hitting the deadline. In a separate research study, group estimates were even more optimistic and inaccurate than individual ones.

Want to know how long it will take you? Ask a friend who has no stake in making it happen.

The mind's eye

For some of us, the process of planning is boring and so we give up. Or we get bogged down and we lose our way - and then give up. If either of these describes your experience, then visualisation, or total immersion planning, may suit your tastes perfectly.

People have used visualisation for years. Sportspeople in particular find it invaluable when preparing for events. Steve Redgrave, the five time Olympic gold medal winner, uses visualisation, and Carl Lewis, the sprinter and long jumper who holds the record for the most gold medals, prepares by putting himself into a floatation tank and visualising each step of the race he is about to face. Goal kickers in rugby teams also use visualisation exercises, injured footballers are encouraged to put themselves through mental workouts, and dancers regularly rehearse complicated choreography in their heads. In terms of improving performance, visualisation is considered by many to provide as much benefit as physically rehearsing the activity.

It works like this: when we visualise ourselves involved in an activity there is almost as much activity in our brain as there is when we are actually doing it. When we visualise ourselves working towards our goals we are doing more than simply daydreaming about the experience. We are preparing neural pathways for the time when we perform the activity for real.

Interestingly, if we visualise only the outcome - that is to say achieving our goal, accepting the Booker Prize, lifting the Wimbledon trophy over our heads, or whatever - the likelihood that we will succeed actually decreases. This is because we then tend to ignore or forget about the effort that we will need to make. We are more likely to assume that, because we have imagined the outcome, it will happen largely of its own accord.

For our chances of success to increase, we need to imagine the steps along the way as well as the outcome.

Warm up

Dream believer

Take a pen and a clean sheet of paper. Place the pen in your non-preferred hand and write your name in the space here:

Now you are going to relax for a while so get comfortable in your chair and close your eyes. Tense all your muscles and then let them go. Screw up your whole body and mind as if you are compressing it into a tiny area and then release it and feel the tension melt into relaxation. Use an image to represent your tension and then let that image disappear: a balloon deflating, a picture fading to grey, a shape dissolving into air. Now breathe in and as you do so let your diaphragm expand. Hold the breath for a couple of seconds, and then exhale. Repeat this with a couple more breaths.

Keeping your eyes closed, visualise yourself sitting in the chair. Picture how you look and what is around you. Imagine turning around and picture what you can see from that position.

Next, imagine you are writing your name with the hand that you don't normally use. Imagine that you are writing it perfectly. See the letters as they are formed in front of you; the curve of an 'e', the circle of an 'o', the straight, vertical line of an 'l'. Imagine the movements of your hand. Imagine how you are holding the pen. Imagine the feel of the pen, its weight, and its shape.

Slowly relax and then begin to come out of the relaxation state. Slowly open your eyes. Now pick up the pen and write your name using the hand that you don't normally use. Write it next to your first attempt.

Is there a difference? Around three quarters of people see a discernible improvement in their handwriting after having visualised the process. The rest improve after repeating the visualisation exercise a few more times.

See the way

Immersion planning, or using visualisation to prepare, uses the same technique but is a little more complex. It consists of five steps:

Step 1: Set the goal

Step 2: Design the path to get there

Step 3: Meet the advisers

Step 4: Refresh the path

Step 5: Write it up (unless we choose to do this as we go along)

Step 1 - Set the goal

The most successful visualisation begins with a clear picture of our ideal outcome.

Think of an issue that you would like to resolve or a goal that you want to achieve. Choose something that represents a bit of a stretch for you, but isn't impossible (getting up tomorrow morning would not, for most, be a stretch and finding life on Mars is not realistic). Name your goal.

Imagine yourself achieving the goal. What do you see? What can you hear? Allow yourself to become immersed in the moment of achievement. What do you feel?

Step 2 - Design the path to get there

Now consider the steps you took to get to this goal. Start with the final step and work backwards until you have reached the first step. Take your time over this - imagine each step along the way as fully as you can. As you do this, you are creating the path to your desired outcome. You may find yourself unearthing elements of the journey that you had not considered before. That's the advantage of working with the end in mind; we are likely to create a more thorough and realistic route.

Step 3 - Meet the advisers

At this point create two advisers to help you with the plan: the expert and the helper. You will use them to help you focus your thinking and to temper any over-optimism that you might be tempted to indulge in. Their role is to ask useful but challenging questions about what you are trying to achieve. The first person you meet is the expert.

The expert

The expert is a character who has some kind of objective knowledge about the situation. Their role is to be logical and unemotional. They'll cut to the quick and ask pertinent questions about how something will be solved. They are not concerned about your motivation and getting you going, they are concerned with the facts. They will search out loopholes in the plan and they'll consider its weak points - they'll put it through the stress test. The expert also gives advice and explores ways in which the plan could be improved or amended.

How you visualise your expert is up to you. Anyone from Einstein and Ghandi to Susan Sontag, Miss Marple or Poirot, it's your choice.

The expert:

- is wise and respected

- is an authority

- is objective and unbiased

- is logical and analytical

- provides an overview

- challenges the thinking

Allow yourself to visualise meeting this person and posing questions to them. The type of questions that you might ask the expert are:

- How have others managed this goal?

- What is the biggest obstacle that I am likely to have to overcome?

- What similar things have you done in the past? Given that, how long do you think it will take?

- What could go wrong, what will not work, what will fail?

- How should I overcome the obstacles?

The helper

The next person you meet is the helper. Their role is very different from the expert. They know you well, they are interested in you and how you will achieve your goal. They are aware of all your foibles, your idiosyncrasies, your strengths and your weaknesses. Some people use a family member as their helper - someone who cares but is going to tell it like it is - or an old college professor or a colleague whom they respect.

The helper:

- is sympathetic

- is completely trustworthy

- has your best interests at heart

- doesn't know any more than you about the goal you are pursuing

- knows you well and may refer to similar situations in your past in order to find the best way forward in your current situation

Questions you might ask the helper include:

- How can I get support?

- How should I approach this?

- Why do I feel this way about the goal?

- What do I need to be mindful of?

- Is this really what I want?

Step 4 - Refresh the path

Having spent as long as you need questioning your expert and helper, return to the step-by-step path that you imagined at the beginning of your visualisation. In light of these conversations how have the steps changed?

Finally, leave the state of visualisation slowly. Allow yourself to become more aware of your environment and the people around you. Open your eyes and take a deep breath. Reflect for a moment on the experience that you have just had, and then, before you do anything else, write it down.

Step 5 - Write it up

Having visualised the plan, it is important that you now write it up. (Some people prefer to take notes as they go, others record their thoughts and a few even ask a colleague or friend to interview them and write down the main points so that insights at the time don't get lost.)

A few tips for a useful write-up:

Make the plan specific

Spell things out in detail, not vague generalisations. This is your map; make it as detailed as you can.

Time and deadlines

Make sure that tasks are matched with time - both in terms of when something is going to happen and how long something will take.

Spare time

Add some time for rollover and spill. However accurate you believe you are, the future will always be sprinkled with the unforeseen. Spare time helps deal with the unexpected without knocking everything else off track.

Include rewards

Your helper may have suggested that your motivation could flag along the way. What can you include to reward yourself when you've achieved something significant?

Cluster tasks

If you can group similar tasks together and do them at the same time, you can save time and be more efficient. So, for example, if you know that you regularly travel by rail, check out the details for all your journeys in one hit rather than repeatedly revisiting the same website to check timetables.

And now you're done.

Your turn

Start with clearing your mind and getting relaxed. Tense your whole face and body up as much as you possibly can, then slowly relax until all your muscles are completely loose. Repeat this a couple of times, each time relaxing that bit more.

Now you are ready.

1	The first plan	
A	Think of an issue that you would like to resolve or a goal that you want to achieve. Use something that will be a stretch for you but not impossible. What is it?	
B	What questions would you most like to ask them?	
C	Imagine now that you are that expert. See yourself in the role and be aware that you have full knowledge of the challenge. What does it feel like?	
D	What are your answers to the questions?	
2	The expert	
A	You meet an expert who can help you with your challenge. What are they like?	
B	What questions would you most like to ask them?	

C	Imagine now that you are that expert. See yourself in the role and be aware that you have full knowledge of the challenge. What does it feel like?	
D	What are your answers to the questions?	
3	**The helper**	
A	You meet a helper who wants to help you with the challenge. What are they like?	
B	What questions would you most like to ask them?	
C	Imagine now that you are the helper. What does it feel like?	
D	What are your answers to the questions?	
4	**Returning to you**	
A	You are now yourself again. How do you feel?	
B	What have you learnt about yourself and how to address your challenge?	
C	What practical steps will you now take to address your challenge?	
D	Leave the state of visualisation slowly, relaxing, reflecting and gradually becoming more aware of the room and people around you. What do you think of the visualisation process? How, if at all, might you use it in future?	
5	**Write up your plan**	

Walt's plan

Walt Disney was famous for his approach to planning and problem solving. It was said that you could never be entirely sure which 'Walt Disney' would arrive at your meeting, because his mood and mindset could change so dramatically.

From interviews with Walt's colleagues, the psychologist Robert Dilts put together a model of the way he thought and planned. It seems that Walt Disney had a whole cast of helpers in his head, which Dilts identified as his different 'modes'. The first was the dreamer mode - where ideas were generated and anything was possible. He'd then move into realist mode, where he'd think about how his plan could be turned into action. At other times Disney would be in critic mode where he'd critique his plan and attempt to mitigate risk and make the plan more robust. If necessary, he'd go back to dreamer mode and start again.

Lovable lists

One quick, easy and sure-fire way to save time is to make a list. Like a pair of Wellington boots, to-do lists may not be sexy but they are highly practical. The very act of writing the list can help us to order our thoughts and stop us from getting bogged down. With an efficient to-do list we remove the need to carry everything around in our head; it's rather like having a back-up drive for our mind. And they show us the big picture, enabling us to see with one glance where we are with a project.

With a smart list, forgetfulness, a major time waster for many of us, can be banished once and for all. There are, however, three rules that we need to follow if we're to get the maximum time gain from our to-do list:

1 **Only one list with everything on it**
It's impossible to decide priorities quickly or accurately if we can't see all the options.

2 **It is always up to date**
If it isn't accurate it's pretty useless, rather like yesterday's newspaper.

3 Each item is expressed as a single action
'Call Alfred', 'Bake cakes', 'Fit fire alarm'; rather than: calls, cooking, safety.

The best to-do lists are highly customised. This can be done by dividing the items into categories, for example: marketing, client, team, personal; or, equipment, medical, supplies, transport. You might want to add a column for 'When I Have Time' (ideal for converting dead time, see chapter L). A 'Waiting For ...' section can also be useful for keeping track of things that other people have agreed to deliver.

Love your list

If the to-do list seems like too much of a chore it won't get used, so it may be worth splashing out on a gorgeous notebook, Blackberry

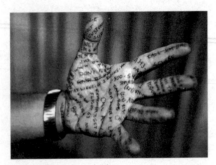

A hands-on to-do list

or PDA. Choose something that you are happy to have with you all the time. This way items can be added as soon as they come to mind and, when we complete a task, we can update straight away. An out of date to-do list is no good to anyone.

A few of the reasons why comprehensive to-do lists do so much good:

- Our mind is freed from remembering what we have to do and so we can get on with actually doing the things that matter.

- We are less likely to forget important or urgent tasks.

- We can quickly and easily decide on priorities.

- We are less likely to get distracted by things that don't matter.

- We worry less and feel more in control because we know the size of the challenge.

- We get the satisfaction from ticking off our achievements, which though minor can help spur us into action.

- We have a record of what we have done, which can be uplifting, especially when we think the day disappeared.

- When we're stuck with, apparently, nothing to do, we can easily find something worthwhile to get on with.

Be prepared

'Life is what happens when you're busy making other plans'
John Lennon

Pad it out

Plans inevitably go wrong from time to time. And so, as well as giving the project a head start with good preparation, the smart planner also has a contingency plan up their sleeve. A simple way to do this is by 'padding' your plan.

- Pad out time to the schedule
- Pad out resources
- Pad out budgets
- Distinguish 'must haves' from 'would like to haves'

If you are planning in a group and people want to take out the padding, fight for it or find a way to protect it. One commercials producer talks about putting in two layers of padding - a visible one and a hidden one. The visible padding can be debated and, if necessary, removed. The hidden layer he keeps in place, ready to deal with the unexpected.

Use scenario planning

With scenario planning we prepare for a number of different possible outcomes by thinking them through fully in advance. There are a number of reasons why this is beneficial:

- It means we are well prepared. If we have several plans (or imagined scenarios) there's a greater probability that the reality will be similar to one of the scenarios.

- It adds flexibility. The process of imagining different scenarios and their consequences enables those involved to be more flexible when the reality takes an unexpected turn.

- It gives us a choice. Having assessed a series of options, the group is more likely to choose the most beneficial, rather than simply acting on the first idea.

'People who make plans make God laugh.' Anon.

It's certainly true that life doesn't always pan out according to our plan - but that is all the more reason to make one. Having a destination in mind equips us to make informed decisions when unforeseen circumstances force a change in the route. A good plan backed up by a flexible attitude will enable us to deal with the unexpected. And in the quest for more and better time, it is invaluable.

Taking command

If time is running through your fingers, you need to take action and close your hand.

Yes, it's time to fight back and this section is here to help. Here is a toolkit of practical tactics that equip us to defeat the toughest of time predators.

First up, a buoyancy aid to prevent us from drowning in the sea of too-much-to-do: K, Over-committed. Next, a miracle cure that will breathe life into the most moribund of moments: L, Dead time. Then, techniques to get rid of those two pernicious, pesky time parasites: M, Interruptions, and N, Persistent offenders. There's also a magic word that will immediately dispense with time demons: O, Saying No and being loved for it. And finally, to tame those tedious tomes, P, A quick read.

For those on a mission to conquer time and make it their own, this is the essential kit.

(K) Over-committed

The solution to being over-committed comes in two parts: cure and prevention. The remedy for prompt relief comes first as it is usually more urgent, but for those who don't want to be repeatedly treating their over-committed ailment, the real gems are in part 2.

Part 1 - Cure

This section consists of four elements:

- Gauging the size of the problem (optional)

- Gaining focus

- Action to reduce the load

- Troubleshooter

Gauging the size of the problem (optional)

When we feel snowed under it can be tricky to tell between a passing shower, a blizzard and an avalanche.

A practical and helpful first step is to assess the size of the crisis. Have we taken on twice what we can manage, four times as much or 'only' one and a half times?

If you feel that you are too over-committed to face a practical exercise right now, skip to step 2. If not, grab a piece of paper and do the following:

- Pick a time frame (eg, next 48 hours or two months).

- Write down all the goals or things you want/need to achieve in that time frame.

- For each goal, list the main tasks.

- For each of the tasks make an estimate of how long it will take.

This is the hardest bit to get even roughly right. To assess the time needed for a task you would do well to:

- think through how long something similar has taken in the past

- ask someone else if they agree with your estimates

- add 20% to all initial estimates as a matter of course

 If this grid doesn't give you sufficient space make a larger one or use the online version.

Time frame:

Goal	Tasks	Time required (hours)
1		
2		

Goal	Tasks	Time required (hours)
3		
4		
Total time:		

Add up the total time needed and divide it by the time you have available and express it as a percentage. The challenge now is to get it down to 100%, give or take 10%.

Gaining focus

What time horizon do you want to focus on?

Picking a specific time period helps us focus. When we're deeply over-committed the shorter the time period, the better. Thinking about the whole year ahead will be daunting and by concentrating on just this week we are more likely to regain our sense of control.

What are your primary goals for this period?

What do you want to have achieved within this time; not every single thing but all the main ones? Write them down.

What is most important?

Of all your primary goals which ones are really important? Suppose you have got a project at work that you feel you have got to finish, but it is also your son's first concert at school. You can't do both this evening: you've got to make a choice. Write down up to three of the most important goals from your list in question 2.

What is most urgent?

Urgent things need doing as soon as possible. They may be the same as the important items, they may be different. Urgent items are things you can't put off, where the consequences of leaving them would be negative. Write down up to three of the most urgent goals from your list in question 2.

Action to reduce the load

Anything that isn't urgent or important will need to be deferred so let's concentrate on the most important and the most urgent goals: a maximum of six.

With each goal, look at what you actually need to do and ask:

- What do I need to do now?

- What could I delegate?

- How can I diminish the time required to complete the task?

- What can I defer until later? (And with whom will I need to re-negotiate?)

- What can I delete from my to-do list altogether? (And who will I need to say 'no' to as a result?)

Fill in the following grid (also online).

A participant who attended a workout on time arrived feeling totally overwhelmed. When asked what he had on he replied, 'Getting married, moving house, completing professional exams and launching a new product line.' Having done step 1 he discovered that his time was 230% committed. It became clear to him that attempting to do all of his priorities inevitably meant doing none of them well. In his case, the activity that was most easily postponed was moving

TASK: Do now Delegate Diminish Defer Delete	TASK: Do now Delegate Diminish Defer Delete	TASK: Do now Delegate Diminish Defer Delete
TASK: Do now Delegate Diminish Defer Delete	TASK: Do now Delegate Diminish Defer Delete	TASK: Do now Delegate Diminish Defer Delete

house which he duly did. He also delegated some of the wedding preparation, diminished his role in the new product launch and took an intensive coaching course for the professional exams. As a result, his life was still hectic but at least this way it became manageable.

Troubleshooter

Here are some frequent problems and responses.

All my tasks are urgent, important or both

Aren't they always? Otherwise they are unlikely to be on our task list. Try rating them in terms of comparative importance and urgency. If you feel the tasks aren't comparable then consider the consequences

The Pareto principle

In 1897 the Italian economist Vilfredo Pareto noticed that 80% of property in England was owned by 20% of the population. Subsequent economic studies looked at other countries and found that a similar ratio applied. Since then the principle has been applied in a wide variety of situations from education theory to the analysis of traffic flow and patterns of criminal behaviour.

The principle states that 20% of effort will yield 80% of the results. It can be a useful prompt when deciding what to diminish.

of not doing each - this helps concentrate the mind on what's urgent and what's important.

I've still got too much on

Go through the cycle once more. This time be tougher. If items can't be removed, perhaps they can be diminished. Is there a way in which you can deliver a good result without having to do the task in full? Still got too much on? Then repeat the exercise over again - as many times as you need to, until you have cut your commitments down to a manageable size.

The tasks I've got on can't be broken down

Take another look at them and think creatively - most things can be reduced to component parts. Are you imposing unnecessary rules on yourself? Do all the parts of the task have to be done at the same time? Alternatively, can you delegate the whole thing?

I don't want to delegate some of this stuff

Then defer it or diminish it. If you can't do either then it will have to replace something else as a priority. The things we find hardest to delegate are those we know (or believe) we will do better than other people. Use this as an opportunity to coach someone up to a sufficient standard and it will be far easier to delegate next time.

People will be upset that some of these things won't be done

It'll be worse if they expect something and don't get it. Managing expectations is half the challenge. It's usually better to be up front

about when you're going to get round to a job than to communicate only when the deadline has passed. Setting a realistic time frame will take the pressure off everyone.

Part 2 - Prevention

The secret to prevention lies in spotting those semi-conscious beliefs that make us want to be busier but for no obvious good reason. Here are a few common ones that you may have spotted in other people. And they may just have spotted in you.

My diary's bigger than your diary

'Well, I've got a brief window at 6.05 for 10 minutes and after that we're looking at the 14th, though even that's filling up. Maybe I could shift Simon to 4.30 and fit you in after that, if you don't mind meeting me on the station platform - or how about a conference call at 5.30? Yes, in the morning.'

Some of us use our bulging diary as proof that we are important, whether to other people or just to ourselves. This is particularly the case in corporate life where, in the power games of executive politics, the diary is one of the primary weapons. The fuller it is, the more power it packs.

The problem is that being busy quickly becomes an end in itself. As soon as we have a free moment or a chance to breathe, we rush to fill it with something - anything, even the wrong thing - just to show how busy, and therefore important, we are.

One way to crack the habit is to look at the evidence. You may be pleasantly surprised to find that many successful people are often not busy at all. Conversely, very busy people often aren't successful (though they might be if they weren't so busy).

It's also worth reminding ourselves that we see successful people only when they are in the midst of activity, which doesn't mean that they are all the time.

A friend of The Mind Gym who was starting up a business, complained that she had no chance of succeeding because she didn't work as hard as other entrepreneurs. When asked, 'how do you know this?' she admitted that it was just an assumption and that she had no real idea how hard other entrepreneurs worked.

The truth is that making ourselves busy to impress others - or ourselves - isn't the key to success but it is the key to being consistently over-committed.

How could I possibly?

Eric Berne introduced the idea of psychological games, meaning unhelpful patterns of behaviour that we use repeatedly with other people. Once we can recognise these games we can stop playing them and so make our relationships more fulfilling and, amongst other things, our timetable less fraught.

Over-commitment is the inevitable consequence of a game called 'Harried'. In this game, the player says yes to every request that comes their way:

Person A: Can you collect the car from the garage?

Person B: Sure.

Person A: And call into the bookshop to pick up my order?

Person B: No problem.

Person A: We don't have anything for supper …

Person B: OK, I'll go to the supermarket.

Person A: And the computer printer is playing up, could you take a look at it?

Person B: It would be my pleasure.

Person A: Sarah wants to know if you would get some stamps from the post office.

Person B: Consider it done.

Person A: And you'll be at the station to pick me up at 6?

Person B: I'll be there.

What a helpful person. Until the time comes for delivery, that is. Impossibly overloaded, this person has set themselves up to fail - but that's not how they will see it.

Person A: Did you manage to get the stamps?

Person B: Of course I didn't get the stamps! How could you possibly expect me to get the stamps with everything else that I have on? And you can forget about being picked up from the station because I didn't get the car, and you are going to have to do without your printer - and supper. I really don't have time to do all this.

In the 'Harried' game a busy person overburdens themselves to the point where they consider they have earned the right to refuse to deliver anything. Sometimes another person plays along with them, adding to the list of tasks and admiring their capacity, whilst suspecting that they will fail to deliver.

As with all these kinds of game, once you're in it, it's hard to get out. So, if you think you have a tendency to play Harried, make an effort to stop it before it starts.

I'm so popular

A business coach recalled how, when she started out, she would work very hard to give her clients insightful advice at their first meeting. They appeared to value her views enormously and on her next visit would present her with a list of new challenges to solve. This she took as a very positive sign and would continue to give the best advice she could. In some cases, this carried on for years.

'It was very flattering,' she recalled. 'There were these high flying business people eager to hear my views.' It was only after a while that she realised that she was making them dependent on her which was the opposite of what an ethical and effective business coach should do. She changed tack and in following meetings she limited herself to one statement for every three questions she asked. This way her clients were forced to work out the solutions for themselves and so, increasingly, they didn't need to rely on her advice. Whilst the frequency of her visits to individual clients declined, the referrals soared; as, for that matter, did her fee.

When we kid ourselves that being in demand is proof of being popular, we run the risk of making things worse by making other people dependent on us - usually without noticing that we are doing it.

If your team always has a long list of decisions waiting when you return from holiday, or your family will only eat ready-meals when you take a weekend away, then you will recognise the symptoms. In the end, nobody gains. Encouraging people to run you into the ground is an exhausting way to make yourself feel loved. It doesn't nurture relationships, either. If you're always too busy to talk to your friends they won't feel valued for long.

Crack the habit by spotting where you are creating dependent relationships and look for ways to help others become self-sufficient. Beef up your delegation skills so that you can build confidence and capability amongst your colleagues (see chapter R, Off load). Or if it's your sympathetic ear that's needed, listen, but then help the person to solve the problem themselves, rather than doing it for them. That way they won't need so much of your attention next time.

Emptiness

For some of us, the sensation of having nothing to do is distinctly uncomfortable. We don't really enjoy being alone with our thoughts and, as a result, down time is just that - time that brings us down. We then fill our diary to beyond bursting point to avoid the more worrying alternative: being stuck on our own.

The way to avoid this is to learn to love time by ourselves. Consider time alone as a luxury which offers a chance to dream, reminisce, reflect on the whys and whats of today's adventures, ponder tomorrow's priorities, or just let our mind drift. As Professor Guy Claxton suggests, *'If your mind keeps wandering there are times it may be wiser than you are. If it wants to go somewhere, get interested in why and where and discover something new about yourself, rather than set up a struggle.'*

Can you smell burning?

Feeling over-committed once in a while may be a natural consequence of an exciting life. But doing it all the time is dangerous.

Burnout is what happens when we reach the end of our tether. It's a combination of physical, emotional and psychological exhaustion and it is often a result of being chronically over-committed. In a recent survey 25% of respondents reported that long hours had a negative effect on their job performance, and 10% felt that their personal relationships had suffered.

The early warning signs for burnout are a sense that our work has no meaning, a mood of helplessness or despair, and a feeling that there is nothing we can do to bring us happiness or success.

Are you burnt out?

Answer each question in terms of frequency

	Never	Only once or twice	About once a week	A few times a week	Every day
I feel that my work drains me emotionally	1	2	3	4	5
I seem to treat people like objects	1	2	3	4	5
I feel exhausted and fatigued at the beginning of the day	1	2	3	4	5
I have become more callous and devious at work	1	2	3	4	5
I feel I am working harder than others at work	1	2	3	4	5
I think the job is hardening me emotionally	1	2	3	4	5
Working with others is a real strain	1	2	3	4	5
I don't care what happens to this company and those who work for it	1	2	3	4	5
I feel pretty much at the end of my tether	1	2	3	4	5
I believe many colleagues blame me for their problems	1	2	3	4	5

A score of over 40 indicates that you are at or near burnout.

And another thing

One other vital tool in the battle against being over-committed is the ability to say No and be loved for it. This is a big subject and merits a whole chapter to itself - chapter O.

(L) Dead time

In 1983, the Bank of England finally called an end to the folding pound note and replaced it with a shiny little pound coin. Since then, over 1.7 billion of these coins have been minted and, of those, 300 million have gone missing. That's the equivalent of 40,000 pounds a day disappearing between sofa cushions and hiding themselves in the lining of coats. That's a lot of pounds. Some, of course, will have opted for early retirement in piggy banks and others may be languishing under mattresses waiting for a rainy day, but all of them have become effectively worthless. No longer available for use they have become dead money.

Something similar happens with time. It doesn't roll under the fridge, but it becomes just as worthless as if it did.

Dead time - as the name suggests it's not the most enjoyable, productive part of our day. In fact, in an imaginary Dictionary of Time, its definition would probably look something like this:

Dead Time *Daid Tame* (n.) from the Latin Morbidus Temporalis **1.** Time that is rendered moribund by either external or internal reasons, that could better be used for other purposes. See also Paint, watching it dry, and Kettle, waiting for it to boil.

Not to be confused with down time, which can be useful and restorative, dead time describes those occasions when we suddenly find ourselves grinding to a halt with nowhere to go and nothing to do. It's not that we've cleared our in tray or achieved all our goals, it's that something or someone has put the brakes on the progress of our day. Our time has got out of our control and become useless to us. Often we don't even notice it happening.

How much dead time is there in a day? It varies from person to person but there is almost certainly more than you think. And if you are a time hungry person, restoring that lost time can make a big difference to your day. Like that forgotten £20 note that turns up in your jacket pocket, reclaiming the moribund moments can provide a welcome time bonus. So take it, it's yours.

The hunt for lost time

Dead time is time that is stolen or lost. Sometimes it is taken from us, other times we give it away. And because this often happens without our noticing it, the first step is to become aware of how much dead time we have in our day. See if you recognise any of these common examples.

1   Hanging on

'We will now transfer you to the main menu. Please press one to be told that all our operators are busy, press two to be told that your call is important to us …'

It could be the phone bank, the council office, the airline, or the cinema ticket queue: they all sound pretty similar. On the surface it may seem merely boring but don't underestimate the power of this particular phone pest. Having stayed on the line for ten minutes, we find ourselves loath to hang up and waste the time we've already spent waiting. So, we hang on and hang on, and whilst we hang on we listen to something that might once have been Mozart, played on something that might once have been a violin, and the longer we wait the more determined we become to see it through, because now we've realised that we are paying for the call too and surely it can't be that much longer and …

You get the picture.

2   Grinding to a halt

The signal failure, the 'earlier incident', the leaves on the line, the wrong kind of snow, the cancellation due to lack of staff, the snarl up at the interchange, the roadworks, the snarl up at the interchange (again), the temporary traffic lights, the diversion, the lane closure, the updated timetable, the weather.

And there are plenty more - so many different reasons to find ourselves going nowhere whilst the time ticks by.

3   Checking out the check-in

You're taking a flight and an early check-in leaves you with time to spare. Luckily - or perhaps not - the airport provides you with plenty of ways to fill it: a newspaper and a couple of glossy magazines, perhaps? A cup of coffee, a snack, a trip to the bookshop, then how about some perfume or jewellery and something shiny and hi-tech to play with on the plane? Time flies when we're having this kind of fun - it's only much later when we realise how much of it we've lost.

4   Waiting-room blues

The dentist. The restaurant. A company headquarters. They may rename their waiting rooms as 'reception areas' but the purpose is still the same: to make you wait. Some of them are, of course, blissfully efficient, but unfortunately they're the minority. In most cases, whether you are fifteen minutes early or bang on time, you're going to come to an abrupt halt when you hit the front desk. You'll be ticked off a list, invited to take a seat and assured that someone will be with you shortly. The receptionist will make a call, announce your arrival and then … nothing. Five minutes, ten minutes, go by. If you're lucky, they've got some goldfish to watch while the minutes slip away.

5   He won't be long

The phone rings at work. You can see from the display that it's someone you've been trying to get hold of for a while, but you're on your way to a meeting so you leave it to the answer phone. When you arrive at the meeting room, prepared and ready to go, a head pops round the door to tell you that the schedule is overrunning by ten minutes. The person you are meeting sends her apologies. She'll be there soon. Which is great, except you're there now, with nothing to do.

Or maybe you're at home, waiting for a washing machine to be delivered. You've never met this particular deliveryman, but you're fairly sure he must be American because his concept of morning is about five hours behind yours. And if you even think about leaving the house in a mercy dash to the corner shop for food, you know they'll be a 'whilst you were out' note waiting for you when you get back.

The above are just a handful of the most common causes of dead time; there are plenty more out there. If you haven't done so already, it is worth spending a few minutes thinking about your own daily routine and identifying where dead time makes a regular appearance in your life (a good use of your time, we promise).

Be prepared

The key to preventing dead time is to have something to do with it. Here is a selection of tools we can carry with us, ready for that moment when the minutes go moribund.

- A to-do list. Check it, there might be something that you could be getting on with - or just thinking about.

- A notebook (paper or electronic). It's bad enough being stuck on a train. But it's even worse being stuck on a train and forgetting the brilliant idea you just had.

- A pen. Worse still is remembering the brilliant idea, remembering your notebook and finding you've forgotten your pen.

- A book. If you never get time to read, here's your opportunity.

- A sketchbook or camera. You never know what might catch your eye.

- Papers to proof or review. Particularly those that don't demand long, uninterrupted bursts of concentration.

- Dull things you've been avoiding. That report you've been putting off, the boring but essential article in the trade press, the small print of your divorce papers. Well, you've got nothing better to do …

I never leave home without it …

A survey amongst workout participants revealed the following time enriching tools: A novel/knitting/sheet music/a massage ball/a poetry book/a sketch book/a chess set/book of meditation techniques/playing cards/a language coursebook/box of magic tricks/crossword/an inflatable pillow.

Keeping your time alive

Having identified some of the troublesome situations, we can now take steps to deal with them. We don't just want to prevent them from using up our time, we're also aiming to turn them into time generating opportunities; situations that are no longer stealing our time, but are also giving something back.

In some cases we're already skilled at doing this. Suppose, for example, you're watching a film you've recorded off the television. What happens when you hit an ad break? Unless you have a particular interest in advertising you fast forward. Over a 2-hour film, there might be eight 3-minute advert breaks: by fast-forwarding past them, we save twenty-four minutes. That's a lot of dead time regained. (Those who watch live and so can't reclaim this time use it to make tea, apparently. Power surges go up during commercial breaks. There are no figures for how many wine bottles are opened.)

1 Hanging on

Rather than allowing ourselves to get stuck in a call centre queue, the simple answer is not to join one. As soon as we hear that the line is busy, put the phone down. Try ringing at a more unpopular time when things are quieter, or use the internet instead. If it's essential to make the call right now, then find something useful or interesting to do while you are waiting.

2 Grinding to a halt

Anticipate the hold-up: take books, audio programmes, electronic chess - whatever you need to keep you engaged and interested. The aim is to turn unexpected delays into opportunities rather than irritants. If you're travelling on a plane, take a project to complete. In the car, have a specific problem to cogitate upon. Driving takes up the right amount of cognitive load to allow the rest of our mind to drift and think very creatively - nuclear fusion was discovered by Leo Szilard while waiting at a traffic light. One workout participant calls their own mobile and leaves messages for themselves with their latest thoughts - hands-free of course.

3 Checking out the check-in

If you fly regularly, then an hour's wait in the departure lounge can quickly become routine. It's a sizeable chunk of time, so why not plan to use it for a longer-term project: learning a foreign language or finally making a start on Proust. With a little thought, departures can take on a whole new meaning.

4   Waiting-room blues

A workout participant explained that he had given up buying newspapers. Instead of tapping his foot impatiently in a client's reception or waiting room, he used that time to catch up with the daily news. As well as keeping him occupied during dead time, it also saved valuable time first thing in the morning - a smart strategy that turns a potential time parasite into a very efficient time generator.

5   He won't be long

There are few things worse than waiting for a meeting because someone else is running late. So plan ahead and make sure you have something to do: perhaps this is a good time to catch up on admin, or read a trade magazine. Similarly, if you're waiting at home for a delivery, make sure you have something productive or useful to do. If you've been meaning to reorganise the wardrobe or sort through the mountain of paperwork, this could be the ideal time to do it. You'll get a tidy wardrobe, a new washing machine, and a warm glow of achievement.

Out of the shadows

The poet Philip Larkin wrote the line: 'Sunlight destroys interest in what is happening in the shade.' Often dead time can force us to slow down and concentrate on the here and now, rather than think about what is coming next. We can let this irritate us or we can welcome it as a reminder to rush less and experience more, a chance to notice things we might have otherwise missed.

Dead time can be a great time to practise mindfulness, to develop our powers of observation, to practise creative thinking techniques or just to dream.

Whatever we choose to do and whatever tools we arm ourselves with, the most important is a mental attitude that says the following: just because this time is being used up unhelpfully doesn't mean I need to let it be. As long as we remember that, we can almost always do something to bring dead time back to life.

(M) Interruptions

Never mind the Porlocks

One afternoon in 1797, the poet Samuel Taylor Coleridge got stoned. He took a dose of opium and, as a result, fell asleep whilst reading about the Mongol ruler Kubla Khan and the fantastical palace that he had ordered to be built. When Coleridge woke, he realised that he had composed hundreds of lines of poetry - lines that were to become one of his most famous poems, 'Kubla Khan'. But the poem we know today is just a fragment of the whole work because, whilst writing, Coleridge was interrupted by a knock on the door and the infamous 'man from Porlock'. By the time Coleridge had got rid of him and sat down to continue writing, he realised to his horror that he'd forgotten the rest of his poem. And so Kubla Khan remains a tantalising glimpse of what might have been.

We might not all be great poets like Coleridge but we all suffer from interruptions. Nowadays the man from Porlock is more likely to turn up in our email in-box or on our voice mail but his arrival is no less intrusive. Along with the phone call that comes as we are sinking into a long, hot bath and the knock on the office door as we are embarking on a tricky conversation, interruptions bring things to a halt and send us off in a different direction. Sometimes, they just slow us down, like a road diversion or a bus replacement service. Sometimes, like poor old Coleridge and his poem, they cause us to lose our thread completely, and we aren't always able to find it again.

The quizmaster of the television show *Mastermind* uses a famous catchphrase to dismiss the interruption of the finishing bell: *'I've started, so I'll finish.'* In this chapter we find out how we can all be in similar control of our everyday interrupters.

Can interruptions be good?

Sometimes, yes. Interruptions can provide a welcome break or an unexpected source of fresh thinking; they can introduce a random element that sparks creative ideas, or space to regroup and re-energise.

'I've started, so I'll finish'

During a 2001 Wimbledon match an interruption proved invaluable for Goran Ivanisevic. Tim Henman was dominating the match and looking set for a place in the semi-finals. Then it started to rain. As the match dragged on from Friday into Saturday and even Sunday, Henman lost momentum. For Ivanisevic, however, the bad weather break provided an opportunity to regroup and he went on to win the championship.

Some interruptions, then, are good, others are irritating, and a few are disastrous. Few of us would want to stop disturbances altogether. What matters is that we feel in control of how, and how often, we are disturbed, either increasing the interruptions when we want more stimulus, or decreasing them when we need more focus.

In the driving seat

When we are interrupted our mental autopilot tends to kick in: we drop whatever we are doing and blindly set about dealing with the new demand. To use the language of psychology, we make 'preconscious' decisions. A friend asks, 'Can you help me out with this?' and before we're even aware that we have a choice, we reply 'Of course, what's the problem?' That's good for our friend. The problem is, it may not be good for us.

Sometimes we have little choice. When an important client piles on the pressure, 'I'll renew the contract but only if you get me the full documentation by first thing tomorrow', we're likely to cancel our plans and get the paperwork sorted. If it starts to rain just as we've lit the barbecue we need to respond quickly, regardless of the fact that our plans had been for a sunny afternoon.

But these examples are relatively rare. Far more often we do have a choice but we act before we give ourselves time to consider it.

In the days before answerphones and voice mail, people would always answer the phone when it rang, even if they were in the middle of something else. The advent of answering machines made this unnecessary. But still many people can't break the habit of rushing to answer the phone before the machine picks up, even when it is inconvenient to do so. We follow similar, often outdated, routines with many other kinds of interruption.

We may also say yes to interruptions because we're bored, or because it is easier than considering an alternative response or simply because we consider it a kind thing to do. If someone asks for something then it feels good to help, especially if there is no conflicting voice urging us to help ourselves instead.

The trouble is that, however valid these reasons seem at the moment, we are storing up trouble for later.

Your own worst enemy

Counter-intuitive as it may sound, you may be the main reason why you get so many interruptions.

Complete the following questionnaire to find out the extent to which you are fuelling or dampening the flow of interruptions. For each of the following, decide on a scale of 1-5 how frequently you behave in this way, where 1=very rarely/never and 5=almost always/always.

When someone interrupts me I …

	A		B
Stop everything and focus on dealing with this new challenge		Ask the interrupter why it needs to be done now	
Do what they want me to do to solve the problem/ address the issue		Ask questions so they work out the solution themselves and won't need me if it happens again	
Get some satisfaction from the feeling of being needed or necessary		Feel annoyed with myself for allowing a situation where I am needed or necessary	
Empathise/sympathise with their problem		Explain the impact that stopping me to address their issue has on me and my priorities	
Once the task is completed, chat about other issues that they want to discuss		Once the task is completed, discuss how to prevent it happening again or promptly return to my priorities	
Carry on discussing other aspects of the issue, even if they aren't urgent		If they want to talk further, suggest they come back at another time	
TOTAL A:		TOTAL B:	

Total up your scores. You should have two numbers between 1 and 30. Now, subtract the score for your first set of responses (A) from the score for your second set of responses (B).

B - A = ____

If your total is a negative number, then you are encouraging interruptions, and the more negative it is, the more you are doing so.

If your score, on the other hand, is a positive number, then your behaviour is discouraging interruptions, and keeping them down. The higher it is, the better you are at doing this.

Usually, those of us who get a lot of interruptions are susceptible to them to start with: eager to help, looking for a diversion, want to feel needed. If we want to change this pattern then we need to change our behaviour. The options in column B are a good start but suddenly adopting these is not easy. Fortunately, there is a technique that can help.

My best interests

There are two types of reaction to interruptions: responsive and agile.

The difference is that when we are responsive we act automatically, usually responding to the interruption as the interrupter would like. When we are agile we make a conscious decision about what is in our best interests. The final decision may be the same, but the difference is enormous. When we are agile, we are in control of how our time is spent, and when we are responsive we are not.

Switching off the autopilot

It's 4 p.m. and we're planning a trip to the cinema with a group of friends. It's a film by our favourite director, with one of our favourite actors and it's had great reviews. Tonight is the last night it's showing nearby. An email pings in; it's a friend pleading for us to come round tonight and help them prepare for a job interview which they've got with our employer. They sound desperate and, as our plans aren't fixed yet (at least we haven't actually bought the tickets), in autopilot we would normally say 'yes'.

Tonight, before we do, we decide to try a new agile technique: PACE.

P = Pause

Freeze the scene. Simply pausing will prevent our auto-response kicking in.

So instead of immediately pressing 'reply' to our friend's email, we take some time to think.

A = Ask

Ask some tricky questions. Test the request from both sides. How urgent is this demand? Who will be affected if we do/don't stop what we were doing before this new demand? What will be the knock on effect?

In the case of our friend's request, we might ask ourselves when the interview is taking place. We check the email again and see that it is not until next week. So there's time to meet up later. That would also give us time to prepare, to read our friend's CV and consider some useful questions. And what about the film? If we miss it, we'll end up waiting for the DVD, we'll be totally out of the loop when everyone's talking about it and we know there are at least a couple of friends who are just as keen.

C = Choose

Decision time. Having considered all the evidence on both sides, we need to decide whether to find for or against the interruption.

We decide to email back asking for a copy of her CV and offering to meet at the weekend. And then book those cinema tickets. Indeed, we might even ask our friend to come along too, it will take her mind off job hunting.

E = Engage

Go for it. Having gone through the previous steps we can act on our decision confident that we have given it due consideration.

We put our plan into action. She isn't nearly as bothered as we had imagined and is quite flattered that we want to look at her CV first, or maybe that's simply because of the confidence we now have about the decision. The film's great too.

We might just as well have decided to cancel the cinema idea and go and help with interview practice. The point of PACE is that it forces us to think things through and make sure we are taking the right decision given the circumstances. It means that we, rather than the interruptions, are in control.

The advantages of PACE

It doesn't need to take long, often just a few seconds.

The more often you use it the easier it is to use. With enough practice it may even become a new routine.

It will surprise you to find how much choice you do have. Even in situations that you thought were inevitable, you can exercise some control.

By using the PACE process you are speaking up for yourself and doing the right thing for you, rather than always letting other people's interests come first.

You will often follow the same course of action as you would have done without the techniques. But if you follow the PACE process you will know why you made the choice. As a result you will feel more in control of what you are doing and how you spend your time.

Drift

All the techniques so far are for interruptions that are external. But what about the ones that are self-generated.

We're in the middle of doing something and then, the next thing we know, it's fifteen minutes later. Where has the time gone? More to the point, where did we go? To our favourite beach, perhaps, or back to last night, to our next meeting, or into that nagging worry that's been distracting us for days.

Drift, those moments when we disengage and float off into our own little world, is an easy way to lose a lot of time. It just tiptoes away, quietly and easily, and often in alarming quantities. Of course, drift is not always a bad thing - reverie and reflection can be great for allowing ideas to stew. What's not so good is drifting off when resolute focus is what we wanted.

Shifting out of drift

The first stage of dealing with drift is to catch ourselves doing it. After all, the quicker we realise we are drifting, the quicker we can right the situation.

We can also pre-empt drift, by learning to recognise the topics, situations and circumstances that repeatedly send us off and either avoid them, change them or keep our drifting antennae especially alert.

Here are four familiar kinds of drift and what to do to make the shift back into focus.

1   My mind is buzzing

Making the shift: If you are distracted because you are trying to do too many things at the same time, take a moment to decide which is the most important task. Do that first. Only when that is finished do you move on to the next, and then the next. The feeling of achievement spurs us on, which in turn will help sustain our focus.

2   I'm fretting

Making the shift: If you can't get something done because you're worrying, then get the worrying done and out of the way first. Imagine it as represented by some physical object, say a stress ball or a bottle of cough mixture. Put all your worries into this object and, once you have done this, put the object away in an imaginary drawer, recognising that you can always get it out again later. Alternatively, give yourself a ten-minute worry time in which to write down all your concerns; then get back to the task at hand.

3   My mind is a sieve

Making the shift: If you're finding it hard to take anything in, then stop. Press the pause button for a while, get up, walk, jump up and down - do something to break the mood. Try sitting in a different position in the room, a shift of perspective can often provide a new energy as well as a new view.

4   I'm bored

Making the shift: Increase the challenge. Either find a task that is more difficult or add a new dimension to this one. A participant recalled that when she studied the Russian revolution for the second time she included as many architectural terms as she could in her essays, as a way of making it more interesting. So, 'Although Lenin was the architect of the revolution, he was building on solid foundations and armed with a blueprint born out of the February uprising ... though the prose of Marx seemed arch to some, the Bolsheviks carved from the ornate fretwork of 'Das Kapital' a simple and classic pediment for the proletariat.'

And so, though it may seem that interruptions are other people's ways of abusing our time, in fact they don't have to be. Drift is, of course, entirely under our control but even the flotsam and jetsam of ad hoc requests can be affected as much by how we behave as how the world treats us.

So we might as well get control of interruptions before they get control of us.

Catching the second wind

By changing the focus or context of a task we can get 'second wind' even when we feel that we are completely out of energy. To demonstrate this, the psychologist Anita Karsten asked people to take part in what she called 'semi-free tasks'. The tasks included drawing, repeatedly writing 'abababababababababab … ', or reading a short poem. The participants were asked to do these tasks until they felt exhausted.

The experimenter then changed the context so that the participant had to do a subtly different task. Those drawing were asked to redraw their last picture to demonstrate how quickly they could draw. Those writing 'abab' were asked to sign their name and address. In this new context their fatigue disappeared. This phenomenon of creating second wind can be seen in action at airports where security officers rotate around different stations to stop routine-induced fatigue settling in.

Give your mind a workout

I TRY When was the last time you responded to a request which put a sudden demand on your time without consciously deciding whether to do so or not?

Pause

What prevented you from pausing? If the situation occurred again, what could you do to make yourself pause?

Ask

What probing questions could you have asked yourself?

What would your answers have been?

Choice

What choice would you have made about the future course of action?

What are the insights from this that you can use next time you receive a new and unexpected demand on your time?

Persistent offenders

My time slipping through your fingers

In our attempt to take control of our time there is one element that is particularly tricky - other people. Friends, lovers, colleagues, family, neighbours: they enrich our lives but they can also eat up our time. If you feel you have a lot of these time munchers in your life it's time to take action.

There are two kinds of people who regularly help themselves to our time.

Firstly, those people on whom we are in some way dependent but who use our time poorly.

The indecisive one

The boss or team leader who is forever changing their mind. Hours of work hit the bin (along with our motivation) as we head towards draft 24 of the report.

The unreliable one

The person who commits to doing something and then doesn't deliver, or delivers something completely different.

The anxious one

The delegator who can't stop checking up on us. They don't seem to realise that all that time spent on progress meetings and outcome reports leaves us with very little opportunity to do the work.

The meandering one

The person who likes to take their time - and ours. Their point takes an age to arrive and their progress is mysteriously slow.

Secondly, there are those people for whom time with us is a better use of their time than it is of ours.

The chatty one

Parent, partner or best mate, this may be a person you love, but why do they always want to talk when you are busy, stressed or otherwise engaged?

The pushy one

The cold call you don't want, the sales visit you don't need. Don't these people have homes to go to?

The needy one

The person who is constantly asking for 'just five minutes of your time' - and then takes an hour.

The controlling one

The person who believes they have a right to chunks of your time. They'll fill up your diary with committee meetings, steering groups, review panels. Whatever their pet project, they want to co-opt you into it.

Do you recognise any of those characters? Most of us have one or two of them in our lives and some have all eight. They may not realise that they are disrupting our time, indeed, the very fact that they continue to do so suggests that they don't. So, if anything's going to change, it's up to us.

Reforming the persistent offenders

It starts with empathy. We need to get inside our persistent offender's head and understand what is driving them. Once we appreciate their needs we can make sure that they get enough of what they want so they give us the time we need as well.

The indecisive one

We're here to help, but best not to say it quite like that. Being too overt is likely to cause upset - are you telling me I don't know how to do my job?

The primary tool in this offensive is the question. Ask, why? What would happen if? How does this fit with other decisions? If they introduce a whole new idea (and experience suggests they might), ask what has changed. Again, perfectly innocently, just so that you can do your job better.

Make it clear that you want to understand what lies behind their decision/request so that if something unexpected happens you can make the right decision without having to interrupt them again. And you want to learn (from them).

This way the indecisive person is more likely to feel helped and supported, you get to work with someone who changes their mind less often, and they feel a warm glow towards you as someone who respects their advice.

The unreliable one

'I've been on a calendar, but I've never been on time.'

Marilyn Monroe

The problem here is that what is a priority for you isn't a priority for them. Your challenge is to make it one.

So, consider their priorities. If you can figure out what makes them tick, you can show how completing the task in question will help them to achieve a goal that they consider important.

The second problem is shifting sands, so when you are starting out on a project with one of these non-deliverers, it is important to be specific. What is expected and by when? Be crystal clear. Wed, 18th at 9a.m., or some time before the end of the day? Is this a hard or a soft deadline? Spell it out and you have removed one of the non-deliverer's most common excuses: Oh I hadn't realised that was what you wanted/when you wanted it.

As the project progresses provide a few gentle reminders, maybe disguised as progress updates. You don't want to slip off their radar but you don't want to become a pest either. Or they won't agree to help again next time.

The anxious one

This is the constant checker who can't leave you alone for long enough to get on with what they asked you to do in the first place. So, what are they worried about? Presumably they are concerned that things will go wrong. And, it seems, they don't yet trust you to deliver what they want.

What to do? Clarify. Make sure that not only do you know what they want, but also that they know that you know what they want. Produce a plan, even if you think it's a waste of time, and show it to them. Get their views on it. It will make them feel comfortable, which is your main priority. Then give them regular updates, so that they feel informed and believe that you're giving it your full attention (whether you are or not).

If you can pre-empt their checking they will begin to feel confidence that you know what you're doing and you won't let them down. They will then turn their attention elsewhere and you will be able to get on largely undisturbed. At last.

The meandering one
Why, oh why, is this person so slow?

A workout participant recalled the story of going to see one of the managers in her organisation. Every question she asked took the man ages to answer. It all sounded so complicated. She kept asking questions thinking that she was being really stupid but when she did eventually connect all the pieces together, the answer to her initial request was pretty straightforward.

It later emerged that this tardy guy took his time because he wanted to seem important. He didn't get many visits from the other managers and so, when he did, he wanted to make the most of it. He also wanted to show that he was indispensable to the business.

The best approach with the slow coach is to address their identity needs. How do they see themselves, and how they want to be perceived? Indulge in a little ego massaging by using a feel good, influencing tactic (also known as good, old fashioned flattery). A little self-deprecation usually helps, too. 'I find it really hard to understand things like this, can you explain it to me in very simple terms?' Whilst you might imagine that this will slow things down as they spell it out in words of one syllable, it may well save time so that you get to the heart of the issue on the first attempt.

The chatty one
One participant recalled getting a postcard with a picture of ET on one side under which was written his legendary strap line 'Phone

home'. On the other, in her mother's immediately recognisable handwriting, was written simply, 'Damn you'.

Another participant recalled the embarrassment of a colleague when she was asked by her husband to talk him through the recipe for a chicken casserole - on the phone, whilst she was sitting in a crowded, open plan office. The comedy increased (for the listeners) as he rang back several times with supplementary questions each time he encountered a new obstacle. Finally, she put the phone down and invited the entire office to join them for dinner - well, she'd wasted their time almost as much as her own.

Bob was a time offender and his jokes were criminal

The best way of dealing with demanding family and chatty chums is to help them realise how busy you are. This doesn't need to be done in a 'look how amazing I am' way. It can just as easily be done with gushing excitement, 'Work is so exciting at the moment, we've just launched a new campaign, and as well as that my boss has asked me to stand in for him at this conference ...'. The more they understand the impact of their behaviour, the less likely they are to abuse your time. We may have to work at this, though; some people need to have it spelt out. So, if you need to tell them exactly what the consequences are, do so. One participant recalled finally stopping his mother's phone calls at work when he said, 'Can I come back and live with you because if we carry on talking much longer, I won't have a job.'

The pushy one
'Are you going to want money from me at some stage? Well I don't have any for you. Goodbye.'

Job done.

This is your phone and your home. Cold callers have no rights to your time and so you need not spend any of it with them.

The needy one
Can I just check this?

What's your advice?

How do I fix this?

What would you do in this situation?

I've finished that; what do you want me to do next?

Why is this person so keen on you? Well, obviously you're a great person with immense wisdom and a sympathetic ear. But what are you doing that's encouraging them to be so dependent? The chances are that it's one of the following, any of which are relatively easy to change.

You are encouraging it. You're flattered that someone is so interested in what you have to say. Maybe they're playing you (daddy, daddy, tell me again about the story when you took on the … can I have some more pocket money?), or maybe they really do rely on what you have to say. Whatever the reason, it's probably not in your interest to encourage these interruptions (in terms of time, it's a pricey way to get your ego massaged). When you appear not to enjoy the requests, the people who are doing it only to flatter will soon stop.

You want to hang on to the reins. Perhaps you need to feel you are in total control and so you require constant updating. Looked at from their point of view you may be acting as The Anxious One. Set up regular reviews - stick to them and try not to interfere in between times. Have a conversation with the other person (who probably isn't keen on all these updates either) and see what you each can do to reduce the amount of time you spend reporting and checking. If you are checking up on them because you are not sure of their abilities, find a way to reassure yourself. Alternatively, you may need to be willing to take a bit more of a risk.

You are not using the right delegation tactic for the job. Needy people have to be encouraged to develop autonomy so that they can deal with future situations without your input. Your challenge is to shift your style of delegation from precision delegation to capability delegation (see chapter R - Off load).

You are solving their problems for them because, well, because they asked you to. Bear in mind you could save time in the future if you coached them to find out the answer for themselves. Instead of pressing the keys to fix their PC problem, tell them what to do and invite them to try doing it while you look on. When people think through the answer themselves they are much more likely to be able to solve similar problems next time.

The controlling one

These are the people who are continually co-opting you to their agenda, their meeting, their lobbying group, their latest pet project. Don't go there. Take control of your diary and make sure that you see only people because you want to - not because they want you to.

Drive your own diary

A newly appointed head of an oil company in Europe arrived on his first day to find that his eager lieutenants had already filled up his diary. In an attempt to reclaim his time he drew a circle to represent all the hours he would have available over his first 3 months. He then split the circle into segments based on how much time he wanted to spend with various groups of people (including some time alone). 10% was allocated to customers, 10% with front line employees, 20% with his immediate team, and so on.

Looking at his diary he found a very different schedule for his time. Most of it was taken up with progress reports from his management team keen to impress their new boss. And so he simply cancelled all the meetings, gave his people log to the lieutenants and told them to re-organise his diary according to the percentages he had written down. Within the hour he was back in control of his time.

Final thought

It's an easy but mistaken assumption to make that a single action will turn the tide. In truth, we won't fix the problem with persistent offenders in one go. By the very nature of them being persistent, the solution is going to be about an ongoing relationship rather than one-off transactions. We need patience to succeed. But if we are clear and keep working at it, we are likely to reclaim control over our time and they are likely to switch to easier prey.

(O) Saying No and being loved for it

For those of us who feel that too much of our time is being taken up by other people, there is one obvious solution: say no.

If only it were that easy.

For many of us 'no' is the hardest word to say, but if we want to regain control of our time we need to make friends with it. Get comfortable with this little word and it will provide you with a simple 'no quibble guarantee' way to more and better time.

Saying no to No

We want to say it, sometimes we need to say it, but somewhere on the voyage between our brain and our mouth, 'No' transforms into 'Yes'. What's going on?

Many of us recoil from 'no' because we feel that there are more important things at stake than our wasted time. We fear the repercussions of this powerful little word. We worry that we might:

- cause offence to someone in a position of power. Better to fritter away my time than risk damaging my career or upsetting a precious client.

- look incompetent or risk-averse. They will think I am saying no because I can't do the job.

- disappoint someone whom we want to like, or even love, us.

- feel guilty. How will I feel if it gets even worse and I wasn't there when they needed me?

- be refused when we make a request in return. Surely the fact that we've said 'yes' means they're more likely to return the favour?

- get into an argument (anything for a quiet life).

Or we may simply think that we will disappoint ourselves. If we equate saying yes with being a good and caring person, refusing a request or rejecting an offer is going to make us feel uncomfortable.

The trouble is that the gain we get from complying is often short-lived. The demands keep on coming and we keep agreeing. We may even get a reputation as a bit of a pushover. And that makes saying no even harder.

And all the while the requests keep eating up our time.

The advantages of No

There are a lot of advantages to saying no occasionally. They aren't always immediate but they can be worth a lot more than the instant fix of capitulation.

Self-esteem

'I used to think that I didn't have the right to say no,' explained a workout participant. 'I thought that other people's views and wishes were more important than mine and so I should just go along with what they wanted. Now I've learnt that I have just as much right to refuse a request as anyone else. And when I have said no, people have listened and accepted what I had to say. As a result my confidence has grown and I feel better about myself altogether.'

Self-control

Who's controlling you? Your partner? Your boss? Your client? It is all but impossible to be in control without saying no every now and then. And given that being in control is one of the three keys to feeling good about time, it's more than a useful technique, it's a necessity.

Reputation

Weak, a 'yes'-man, no backbone, soft touch, easy target, sucker.

Of course, people won't say this out loud but it's what they may be thinking. And when it comes to deciding who has the mettle for the top job, what are the chances of making it even to the long list?

Quality

Creative genius often comes out of fierce debate. Whether it's Lennon and McCartney, Gilbert and Sullivan or Simon and Garfunkel, they wouldn't have become legends if instead of relishing disagreement they'd avoided it. When we say no or, at least, 'no to this as it stands' we open up the possibility of finding something even better.

Efficiency

Saying No makes us more efficient. It means that we are more likely to do only the things that will have the greater impact. No nonsense.

Time

And now to the nub of the issue. The more we agree to requests, the more our diary fills up. And if we are saying yes to things that we do not want or need to do, we are unlikely to feel good about the time we spend on them.

Oh, no

In half an hour it will be Friday evening and the start of the weekend. But not just any weekend.

It's your partner's birthday and you've planned a surprise. You've taken over the local Italian restaurant. When they arrive they are going to find it packed with friends, all eating at separate tables so it will look as if they are there by co-incidence. It's going to be quite some party.

There's an 'ahem' behind your back. You swivel round. It's the head of department. There's a bit of a problem with the office in the States. You glaze over a little as she starts talking about 'data' and 'deadlines' and difficulties 'backing up' but you get the gist of it. Someone has to be in the office this evening and she thinks it should be you. It shouldn't be too long, she says, smiling thinly. No more than a couple of hours. All done by ten at the latest. It means a lot to know that she can count on you, especially in these tricky times when her department's being cut. You can stay behind, can't you?

Things are not looking good. Miss the birthday party, or disappoint the head honcho? Fettucine Vongole or a sandwich in front of the computer screen?

So, how do you get out of this?

Here are three options that should do the trick.

The straight No

The straight no is the simplest and most direct way of saying no. It's an upfront and unambiguous response and reaps its rewards accordingly.

How we deliver it depends on who we are dealing with. Just saying 'no' on its own is fine for someone we don't want to see again (the man with the clipboard asking you to take part in a survey, for example), but for friends or colleagues a little more finessing is required. Use the following three steps to deliver a more palatable refusal.

Reasons

This shows that we have thought about our response and aren't dismissing their request out of hand. If they can see that there is a rational argument behind our response, they will find it easier to accept our rejection.

Empathy

Empathising shows that we acknowledge their position and are taking it seriously. Again it demonstrates our 'no' is considered rather than dismissive. And it makes it clear that this is a refusal, not a rejection.

Alternatives

This shows we care about their interests and want to help. It also makes the refusal specific rather than general: it's just that we can't meet this particular request on this particular occasion for the reason that we gave. It also moves the conversation on from the negative to positive suggestions.

When we put these three elements together we get something that sounds firm and reasonable like this:

No, I'm afraid I can't tonight because it's my partner's birthday and I've organised a surprise birthday party. I do, however, appreciate that someone needs to be here to check that the download is complete. Would you like me to ask around the team and see who could be available? I know that Alex is planning a weekend away next week - he might be willing to stay on tonight if he could leave early next Friday.

The straight no is very useful when the situation requires complete clarity and when the other person is persistent. But if you feel it is a little abrasive for this particular Friday afternoon crisis, there is an alternative.

The soft No

This second way of saying no is a more subtle response: the intent is the same, but it is presented in a different way. The soft no is useful in delicate situations.

Engage but don't answer

Start by making a bridging statement to take the sting out of the refusal and make the situation less confrontational. Acknowledge what the other person has said and concentrate on the elements you agree on, for example 'It's essential we support the States ...' or 'I appreciate that you see me as someone you can rely on ...'

An effective bridge statement is positive and shows that we have been listening, but it doesn't reveal our position. It also provides a link to the soft no.

Introduce the soft no ...

There are four different ways to deliver the soft no:

1 Analogy: Show don't tell

Use an example or an analogy to illustrate why you can't say yes. For example you could refer to a shared experience: *You know how thrilled David was last year when his girlfriend arranged the surprise trip to Florence? Well I'm doing something similar for my partner tonight.*

2 Suggest an alternative

Point out a way of solving the problem that doesn't involve you. The

States can now see what the problem is online. So, if there is a glitch, they could call, and any one of us could explain how to solve it on the phone. I can brief them before I leave. Whose number should I give?

No but nice

Here is a range of options for a soft no developed by a work-out participant. There is no need to work down a column - it's more like a pick and mix, taking one from each row.

Request	Jon, I am looking for a job - do you think that you can possibly get me an interview at your company?			
Bridge	I'm sorry that it hasn't worked out at the current place.	It's difficult finding a job in this market for sure.	I'm so impressed by your persistence in trying to get a job.	You're looking well despite everything.
Soft no	(Analogy) My colleague Nick tried to get his niece an interview the other day but the HR Director said that everyone had to go through the formal channels - no exceptions.	(Alternative) What I can do is help you structure your CV and application letter so that it has the best possible chance of getting you an interview.	(Facilitate) What is it you really want to do? Why do you think that you'd like to work here?	(Context) We've recently lost some people in the department and I would feel bad about being seen to recruit in these circumstances.
Check	I hope you understand.	Shall we sit down and have a look at what you've got?	Is that OK?	Is there anything else I could do to help?

3 Facilitate: Lead them to say no for you

Rather than saying no yourself, get the other person to say it for you: You do know that I haven't been fully trained on the latest server upgrade yet?

4 Put your refusal in context

Elaborate on the principles underpinning why you are saying no: I remember you saying how we should work as a team and support each other. That was why I was happy to stay behind on the last two occasions when we had to sort out the download from the States and I think it is someone else's turn this time.

Check that the message has been understood

Because we have said no without saying no, it is worth making sure that we have got our message across. I'm sure you understand; Is there anything else I could do to help?

The pre-emptive No

Better than even the softest no is getting your answer in before the question has been asked. This makes it much harder for the person to make their request in the first place. Step one is to spot the request that's coming your way.

Active antennae

Be alert and anticipate what might be coming. Listen out for information ('Clare is looking for someone to stay behind this evening') and use your instinct. Read the body language signs. If you see Clare heading towards you with a 'how can I put this well?' expression on her face, get ready to act.

Soften the ground

Now we do the 'no' bit. It's slipped in surreptitiously; a no by implication, if you like. Give the facts (Did you know that I've been organising a surprise birthday party? It's taken weeks to get everything together), and explain why it matters to you (I guess I'm a romantic at heart) and don't be afraid to show your vulnerability (I'm actually rather nervous). Who could ask you to miss the party after that explanation?

Shift the conversation along

Having made it clear that you would have to say no to their unasked question, move on. Change the subject or ask an unrelated question. By the time you've finished discussing the new website pages, or the cricket score, or the restaurant that's just opened nearby, the window of 'asking' opportunity will have passed.

This is how it works in practice:

Your phone rings. You see from the call display that it's a client who's always ringing requesting 'a quick bit of advice'. You know from experience that this usually means he's after a long bit of free consultancy. So, get in quick. *'Hi Simon, good to hear from you. I was just going to send you an email, in fact. I've been doing some work on my consultancy rates - I've been getting worried recently that I'm not charging properly for my time. I seem to be overstretching myself. I'd really value your opinion. Would you take a look over them some time?'*

No, minister

Politicians are notorious for evading questions. But how?

Analysis of the responses of Margaret Thatcher (then Prime Minister) and Neil Kinnock (then leader of the Opposition) in political interviews during the 1987 general election campaign showed that non-replies accounted for between 56% (Thatcher) and 59% (Kinnock) of responses.

Overall there were 30 different kinds of non-reply. Margaret Thatcher was especially keen on declining to answer and attacking the questioner. In response to a question about whether to form a coalition with the Alliance or allow a minority Labour government in the event of a hung parliament she said:

… nothing you say will trap me into answering what I do not believe will happen or trap me into saying precisely how we would react in those circumstances. You know I might indeed, I would consult my Cabinet colleagues the very thing you've accused me of not doing.

Sir Robin Day: *I didn't accuse you of anything, Prime Minister; you keep accusing me of accusing you of things.*

Neil Kinnock's non-replies usually took the form of negative answers, stating or implying that he had already dealt with the point, and dismissing the question. In response to a question on how he would respond to aggression from the Kremlin without a nuclear deterrent, Kinnock replied:

It's the stuff of which novels are made and I don't think it could be or should be regarded as a serious proposition.

Margaret Thatcher's more aggressive techniques were significantly better at moving the interviewer on to a new topic than Neil Kinnock's defensive non-replies which usually led to the interviewer repeating the question.

Unlike Neil Kinnock, Margaret Thatcher would also answer by implication, making her views clear without giving a direct response.

When asked by Sir Robin Day whether, if the Labour Party were elected and they decommissioned the Polaris nuclear missiles, it would be the duty of the chiefs of staff to resign, she stated:

… I know what I would do, I just could not be responsible for the men under me. Under those circumstances it wouldn't be fair to put them in the field if other people had nuclear weapons … but they are free to make their decision - that's a fundamental part of the way of life in which I believe.

She makes her view clear without explicitly saying whether she thinks it would be the duty of the chiefs of staff to resign. Not so different from the soft No.

No nonsense

Whilst there are plenty of excuses for not saying No, there are a lot of good reasons why most of us should turn down more requests than we do. You get the full benefit of agreeing to something only when you also disagree from time to time. The Man from Del Monte's reputation wasn't built by accepting any old orange.

Provided we do so with skill and sensitivity, saying no can win us as many friends as saying yes, and they may well last a lot longer. Even more essential, it is one of our strongest allies in the battle for time.

Still unsure?

Give your mind a workout

SPY Next time you are watching TV, listen out for the different types of soft no.

Whenever you hear it decide which of the following is being used:

- analogy - an example or comparison with another situation where the answer was No.

- alternative - suggesting another way of meeting the need.

- facilitation - using questions which lead the person making the request to discover the No.

- principles - establishing criteria which imply that the answer is No before the question is asked.

Different people have different preferences and some styles are better suited to particular situations. Politicians, for example, often use principles to explain their disagreement. Counsellors, on the other hand, are more likely to use facilitation.

TRY If there is a particular person you find it hard to refuse, or a situation in which you find it difficult to say no, use the following questions as part of your preparation (this is available at The Mind Gym Online with some more advice on how to prepare).

What is the situation?

Why is it difficult to say No?

What are the benefits of saying No? List as many as possible.

Which type of No is most likely to be effective? The straight no, the soft no or the pre-emptive no?

How will you deliver this No? Write down what you would say and check to see that you have covered off all the main elements.

(P) A quick read

'I went on a speed reading course and read War and Peace *in ten minutes. It's about Russia,'* said Woody Allen.

Whilst many of us would love to be able to read faster, we fear that, if we do, we'll miss out. We may skim the words more rapidly but, as a result, we will lose their meaning.

The challenge, therefore, is to increase the pace at which we read whilst maintaining, if not increasing, our level of comprehension. The techniques in this chapter will do exactly that.

When we want to savour the verse of Lord Byron, or relish the prose of Henry James, speed reading techniques are the last thing that we want. For everything else, from dishwasher manuals to encyclopaedias, industry reports to psychology books (especially them), these techniques will help both increase our knowledge and save precious time.

The need for speed

The average person has a reading speed of about 200 words per minute. That's dramatically different from the 4,000 words a minute world record held by an American speed reading champion. The experts, however, are a little sceptical about these sorts of speed - it all depends, they point out, on your definition of 'reading'. If reading is defined as comprehending most of the words on a page then a reasonable upper limit is about 600 words per minute. To get speeds of 4,000 words per minute, people must be simply skimming or scanning the page. One of the more cynical experimenters investigated a claim of 10,000 words per minute and found that the speed readers failed a 20-item multiple choice test even after three readings. In his opinion the only noteworthy skill exhibited was a remarkable rate of page turning.

That was then

The origins of speed reading lie with the Royal Air Force, who wanted to train pilots to recognise aeroplanes from a glimpse. They discovered that people could distinguish images extremely quickly, and wondered whether people could learn to process words in the same way. They found that they could. Since then there has been little looking up with reading aficionados scanning pages at ever increasing rates.

This is now

First, discover how good your reading speed is already. What you need is a stopwatch and a calculator (your mobile will probably be sufficient - no complicated formulas).

Start the clock and read the following piece.

Test 1 - Bambi's got a little secret

We crab and crouch in the brush, low to the ground in the woods of Michigan. Deep, deep in the woods. Patient, silent, dressed as trees, we stalk our prey. Not the mighty bear or the trophy buck but an animal far more dangerous, and dumber than a bucket of rocks. The poacher.

A white pickup skids to a halt, the driver spotting a white-tailed doe and a buck in the brush off Sucker Creek Road in Alcona County. The deer are on private property, so if this hacker grabs his rifle and takes a shot, he's under arrest. Bob Mills, my partner, radios to our backups, Sergeant Pete Malette and Officer Warren MacNeill, who are hiding in a nearby grove. 'We've got a looker,' Mills tells them.

The driver is backing up slowly, so as not to scare the deer away before he can get a clear shot. What he doesn't know, the poor sap, is that the deer are not real. They're robodeer. Yes. Robotic deer. Who can compete with American ingenuity? Malette just had a funeral for a buck that took so many bullets in the line of duty - more than 100 in seven years - they called him Sluggo.

All across the country, conservation officers use mechanical Bambis, most of them made by a Wisconsin taxidermist, to nab poachers.

The deer don't gallop through the woods or eat prize rhododendrons. Only their heads and tails move. But that's all it takes. 'You can't believe the look on a guy's face,' Malette says, when a brawny hunter discovers he has just blown holes in a stuffed animal with AA batteries in its head.

Mills gives me a cue to flick the two joysticks that make my deer's head swivel and her tail twitch from 50 yards away. This would be easier if not for the camouflage hat the officers gave me. With a curtain of dangling burlap strips, it looks like Bob Marley has joined a militia. My doe's head may be spinning around like something out of *The Exorcist* for all I know. I can't see through the dreadlocks. The driver may not know whether to lock and load or call a priest. But he's still watching. Go ahead, tough guy. Show some courage.

Some poachers have argued entrapment, but Malette knows of no one who's got off on that defense, because the typical charge is trespassing, carrying a loaded weapon or shooting out of season, which can cost up to $500 in fines and 90 days in the brig. And he's come across some real All-Stars. The Hemingway wannabe who wet his pants when he got caught. The jughead who was nabbed twice in one day. Malette uses a wild-turkey decoy too, and had one cowboy go after it with a .357 Magnum. We're talking National Rifle Association Dream Team. But the all-time champ was the Lions Club president who asked Malette to bring a decoy to their meeting. 'They were laughing, and the president said, 'Who's going to take a shot at this thing?' Three days later Malette had the decoy on a stakeout. Guy drives up, gets out with his rifle and blasts away. The Lions Club president.

And that was back in the '80s, when the decoys had no moving parts. Brian Wolslegel, the Mosinee, Wisconsin taxidermist, with a former partner began experimenting with moving parts several years ago. He sells 200 to 300 robots a year at about $800 a pop. In the past six years, conservation officers from 45 states and Canada have bought Wolslegel's robotic elk, turkey, deer and bear. Wolslegel glues real animal hides to polyurethane molds, cuts off the heads and installs batteries and robotics, then slides the heads back on. (The very process, oddly enough, that's used to make presidential candidates.) 'I'm backed up about 50 orders right now,' says Wolslegel. He sells almost half the robots to hunters, who use them as decoys.

And I'm backed up deep, deep in the woods of northern Michigan, stalking the ultimate game. I flick my doe's tail and turn her head so she's staring down the guy in the white pickup. A rookie mistake, maybe. So many poachers have been bagged, they're taking a closer look now, and this guy just got wise to us. He hits the gas and disappears. No problem. We're on Sucker Creek Road after all. I crouch. I adjust my dreadlocks. Next guy down the road is mine.

Words per minute

Now it's time to calculate your words per minute rate. Do this using the following equation:

The passage you read was 752 words long, so divide 752 by the number of seconds you took to read the piece and multiply by 60. This will give you your words per minute. Having calculated your reading speed, plot it on the graph at the end of the chapter.

Comprehension

Next, comprehension. Answer the questions below to get a sense of how much of the content you took in.

1   Which American state are they in?

    a   Connecticut

    b   Maine

    c   Michigan

    d   Texas

2   What are they hunting?

    a   Bears

    b   Poachers

    c   Bucks

    d   Rabbits

3   What colour is the pickup that arrives?

    a   White

    b   Blue

    c   Red

    d   Black

4   What sort of deer are they?

   a   Electrodeer
   b   Robodeer
   c   Mechanideer
   d   Roe deer

5   Who makes the majority of the deer?

   a   A taxidermist
   b   A taxi driver
   c   A mechanic
   d   A decoy specialist

6   What defence argument do poachers use?

   a   Engagement
   b   Blackmail
   c   Hunger
   d   Entrapment

7   How much can the fine cost?

   a   £400
   b   £500
   c $500
   d $600

8   What weapon did the 'cowboy' use to shoot with?

   a   .355 Magnum
   b   .356 Magnum
   c   .357 Magnum
   d   .358 Magnum

9   Where is Brian Wolslegel from?

   a   Mosinee
   b   Maine
   c   Minneapolis
   d   Minnesota

10 Other decoys include …

    a   Moose and duck
    b   Elk and turkey
    c   Bear and goose
    d   Horse and chicken

The answers are on page 204. Mark your responses, then plot your score on the graph at the end of the chapter. The average comprehension rate is 70%.

You've now established a base line for your reading. Can you improve on it?

Bad habits

Learning to read quickly is as much about undoing poor habits as it is about perfecting new techniques.

There are three particularly common practices that many of us have acquired and that may be slowing our reading down: subvocalisations, eye control and fixations. Fortunately, there are cures for all of them.

Talking to yourself

Folklore has it that talking to oneself is the first sign of madness. It isn't, in fact it's quite normal, though best to keep the volume down in public places.

The technical name for talking to ourselves as we read is subvocalisation. When we first learnt to read we were encouraged to speak the words aloud so that our teacher could check that we'd got each one right before we moved on. As we mature, we internalise that voice, so we still hear it in our heads. But this inner voice is not necessary in our reading; in fact it reduces reading speed to around talking speed which is around 180 words per minute.

Eye jumps

When we read our eyes jump around the page from one place to another. This is in part because without something to follow, our eyes find it very difficult to keep to the lines on a page.

Find a friend and ask them to picture a large circle in front of them. Ask them then to follow the outline of the circle with their eyes. What you will notice is that their eyes jump from one place to another. Now put your finger out in front of you and ask them to focus on the end of your finger. Trace a large circle. Notice how their eyes move - perfectly smoothly.

This problem occurs when we are reading - our eyes flit from one place to another, either unintentionally or when we believe that we need to reread something.

The pointer
So, how do we get rid of eye jumps and subvocalisations?

One way is to use a pointer. This works by giving the eye something to follow. The pointer can be anything from a pen or pencil to a chopstick. To use it, run the pointer across the page underneath the line you are reading and make an effort not to say the words to yourself as you go. For those who are left handed it might take a little experimenting to find a comfortable way of holding the pointer so that you are pulling your pointer rather than pushing it.

A pointer helps our eyes focus on what we are reading, thereby reducing the number of eye jumps we make. Pointers should be moved across the page as smoothly as possible and always a little faster than you think you can read.

Now let's see how much difference using a pointer and removing subvocalisations makes. Remember, move the pointer a little faster than is comfortable.

Test 2 - The high life of crime

The 'cat' crept stealthily through the night, never letting a twig break or a floorboard creak, now gliding past a Rottweiler snoozing on the lawn, now past a man snoring on a sofa inside, now reaching noise-lessly for a Tiffany soup tureen and depositing it in his duffel, careful not to let it clank against the sterling bonbon spoons. Then away he stole, leaving no trace but the glass panes from the French door, stacked neatly on the patio.

With over 150 burglaries in 10 states, Blane Nordahl was one of the most celebrated cat burglars ever to work the East Coast, making off with $3 million worth of silver from places like Palm Beach, Florida;

the Hamptons on Long Island; Greenwich, Connecticut; and Westchester County, New York. Never armed, never violent, he crept in and out without waking his victims.

But even a cat has only nine lives. On October 27, a federal judge sentenced Nordahl, who was arrested in Baltimore in 1998, to five years in prison on charges of conspiracy to transport stolen property interstate. Already he has spent years in jail, where he still recalls the thrill of a thief's life. 'It's like a natural high,' says Nordahl, 37, a man of disarming candour and utter lack of remorse. 'It fills a void. A lot of times life can be very mundane, very tedious. You want something different.'

Ever since Cary Grant played a suave, darkly handsome cat burglar in the 1955 Alfred Hitchcock thriller *To Catch a Thief*, the notion of men who creep by night into the homes of the rich to steal jewels, artwork, and silver has occupied a special niche in American popular culture. A succession of TV shows from the late 1960s through the 1980s featured variations on the character of gentleman thief.

Real life

But Blane Nordahl is no Cary Grant. He is a 5-foot, 4-inch, 175-pound man with a receding crew cut and a moustache, sitting in the noisy visiting room of a Brooklyn, N.Y., federal prison. And his victims aren't film characters but real people who weep at the loss of family heirlooms.

In many ways, Nordahl is an unlikely burglar. He hates confrontations; he's scared of guns. 'If you carried a gun,' he says, 'there's always the chance you could use it.' He says he won't touch drugs or even caffeine. And he steals only silver. 'Jewellery is in the bedroom,' he says. 'People could wake up.' But what really set Nordahl apart was his meticulous methodology, from his targeting of 'old money' homes to his unerring choice of only the finest sterling - he always left silver plate behind. His ability to skirt burglar alarms even earned grudging respect from the police. 'What he's doing is wrong,' says Detective Sgt. Michael Schucht of the Southampton Village Police Department in New York. 'But of all the burglars I've ever gone up against, he is absolutely the best.'

Using publications as diverse as Sotheby's Preview and the du Pont Registry, as well as real-estate agents and local libraries, Nordahl educated himself about fine silver and classy neighbourhoods, then scouted for homes with older residents. 'People who have newfound wealth are much tighter with their money,' he says. 'They're not going to spend $100,000 on a silver tea set to put on their buffet. They'll buy silver plate.' When Nordahl started to burglarise homes in the early 1980s, he would sometimes climb a utility pole to disable the burglar alarm. Other times, he purposely set off the alarm repeatedly, until the exhausted homeowner finally turned it off. In more recent years, though, he simply bypassed the security system altogether by cutting glass or wood panels out of doors or windows, then avoiding the motion detectors hidden under the rugs. 'Alarms are made and installed by people who are not burglars,' he says. 'They don't see the areas of vulnerability I do.'

Often, the alarms weren't even on, as in the Greenwich, Connecticut, home of retired printing company executive James T. Sullivan. 'We felt secure,' says Sullivan, who noted there had been 'very few robberies' in the area at the time Nordahl struck in 1996. Sullivan's wife had spent 35 years collecting the tea set, candelabra, flatware, bowls, and vases that they displayed in their dining room and planned to pass on to their children. Nordahl stole $40,000 worth that night. After the robbery, Sullivan spent $10,000 to turn the seven-bedroom home into 'an armed camp - [with] everything but the howling Dobermans.'

The scent of fear

Still, even Dobermans don't deter an expert thief. If pets roam a house, it usually means that no indoor motion sensors are on. Nordahl rarely woke the dogs, and when he did, they seldom barked. Dogs smell fear, Nordahl says, and he prides himself on staying calm. One house he entered had seven dogs, recalls Detective Cornell Abruzzini of the Greenwich, Connecticut, police. 'Not one barked.'

Nordahl made missteps, however. In 1995, he broke into Andalusia, the historic Pennsylvania estate of late financier Nicholas Biddle. 'I had a house full of guests,' recalls James Biddle, the current owner, who lives in the guest cottage. 'They were . . . up at 4:30 or 5 a.m. and must have scared him off.' In the morning, Biddle found silver neatly piled by the windows for a hasty exit. But Nordahl wasn't done: A year later, he burglarised Andalusia's 38-room main house, making off with over $100,000 of antique silver, much of it from the early 19th century and marked with the Biddle family crest. (Little of Nordahl's plunder has been recovered; police believe he sold most of it to a fence who shipped it to Europe.)

Nordahl's costliest mistake was a simple one: a footprint on the kitchen counter of a house in Little Silver, N.J., in 1994. The print matched a sneaker police found in his hotel room. After that, Nordahl was in and out of jail several times, committing burglaries between visits. In a plea bargain arranged by attorney Robert W. Eisler, Nordahl admitted to crimes up and down the Eastern seaboard and as far west as Chicago since 1984, allowing local police departments to wipe hundreds of unsolved burglaries off the books. In exchange, he received a relatively light sentence, most of which he's already served.

'He's the kind of guy who could be very helpful if employed by a burglar alarm company,' says attorney Eisler. But Nordahl, a Midwest high school dropout who drifted into burglary after a stint in the Navy, doesn't seem all that committed to rehabilitation. 'His burglaries are like a drug addiction - that's his high,' says Monmouth County, N.J., Detective Lonnie Mason, who spent years chasing Nordahl. Indeed, Nordahl fairly glows when he describes the exquisite silver pieces that have passed through his hands, including 'bowls made by Mr. Tiffany himself.'

'One I'd definitely love to get ahold of,' he says dreamily, 'is an original Paul Revere.'

How did you do?

That piece was 1,159 words. Calculate your reading speed and plot it on the graph at the end of this chapter.

Here's the equation:

$$\text{Words per minute} = \frac{\text{Number of words}}{\text{Number of seconds}} \times 60$$

Comprehension

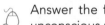

Answer the following questions. If you are unsure, guess, your unconscious mind may be working harder than you realise.

1 How many states did Nordahl operate in?

a 8
b 10
c 12
d 14

2   What is his first name?
    a   Blaire
    b   Barry
    c   Blane
    d   Wayne

3   Where was Nordahl arrested?
    a   Boston
    b   Buffalo
    c   Boulder
    d   Baltimore

4   What doesn't he touch?
    a   Caffeine and drugs
    b   Chocolate and coffee
    c   Cigarettes and alcohol
    d   Burgers and chips

5   What buildings did he target?
    a   Schools
    b   Those belonging to older residents
    c   Old people's homes
    d   Department stores

6   What did he avoid that were hidden under rugs?
    a   Motion detectors
    b   Noise detectors
    c   Booby traps
    d   Heat detectors

7   How much did Nordahl steal from James T Sullivan?
    a $10,000
    b $20,000
    c $30,000
    d $40,000

8   How many dogs slept through one burglary?
    a   5
    b   6
    c   7
    d   8

9 What did he do before becoming a burglar?

   a   He was in the army

   b   He was in the navy

   c   He was in the airforce

   d   He was in the marines

10 How does Detective Lonnie Mason describe Nordahl's burglaries?

   a   As an obsession

   b   As a crime

   c   As abnormal behaviour

   d   As an addiction

The answers are on the final page of this chapter. Calculate your total and plot it on the graph.

Some people find using a pointer difficult, especially if it is travelling a little faster than they think they can read. They also find that their comprehension may have dropped a little. This is usually because they have been thinking, 'I wonder if this is working' or 'this looks silly' or some such, whilst they are reading. If we allow these subvocalisations or even internal instructions to creep in, both comprehension and speed will suffer. We must focus on the text and with practice we usually do.

Fixations

The tinhg aubot raeidng is taht our barins don't foucs on the wohle wrod but on seipfcic ltteers. These specific letters tend to be the first and last, the rest of the word is recognised by our brain and put together for us. One reason our reading speed slows down is because of the number of points we feel we need our eyes to make on a page. We tend to take in every word rather than looking at more than one word at the same time. So rather than fixing on every single word like the sentence below:

1	2	3	4	5	6	7	8	9
The	quick	brown	fox	jumped	over	the	lazy	dog.

we make fewer fixations:

1	2	3
The quick brown	fox jumped over	the lazy dog.

There has been some controversy over how many words we can fixate at any one time. Research has shown that inefficient readers make more and longer fixations than efficient readers and some speed readers claim that they can fixate on entire paragraphs or pages. However the arrival of advanced eye-camera technology has suggested that the maximum fixation is two words on either side of the fixation point.

We still use the pointer to give our eyes a focus, but now we take in fewer fixations as our eyes move along the page.

Here's a third test to have a go at taking fewer fixations. So, get your timer ready and, go.

Test 3 - Europe:
A continent of bizarre sporting endeavour

The Wimbledon Tennis Championships, Euro 2000, the Tour de France, The Six Nations Rugby Competition: Europe has always been a continent of great sporting occasions.

All too often, however, the big sports have tended to overshadow the smaller ones. Tennis, football, cycling and rugby are all very well, but there are a host of other smaller competitions which, while receiving less coverage, are every bit as exciting to watch (or in some cases listen to).

Take the World Screaming Championships, which have recently been wowing audiences (and breaking windows) throughout the town of Goldap in northern Poland. A sort of heavyweight-boxing contest for vocal cords, the championships attract entrants from as far afield as Japan, Austria, the U.S. and the Czech Republic, all battling it out to see who can emit the loudest scream.

Competition this year was especially fierce, with male-screamer Pawel Dabrowski looking set to carry away the prize after producing a career-best performance of 125.3 decibels. That, however, was until middle-aged housewife Dagmara Stanek stepped forward and, to the delight of the crowd, unleashed an ear-shattering 126.1

decibel bellow - equivalent to the sound of a pneumatic hammer - that snatched the championship from right under Dabrowski's nose.

From harrijasotzailes in Northern Spain (large men lifting up stones) to caber-tossing in Scotland (large men throwing logs) to wife-carrying in Finland (large men carrying their wives), Europeans leave no stone unturned (log untossed, wife uncarried) in their determination to find new and imaginative ways of competing with each other.

Finland's sporting heritage

Nowhere is this sense of sporting innovation more evident than in Finland, which boasts more sporting competitions than almost any other country in the world. Here, alongside better known events such as football, skating and cross-country skiing, you will encounter such delights as the World Mosquito-Killing Championship - won last year by Henri Pellonpaa with 21 kills in five minutes - and, of course, the unmissable Air Guitar World Championships.

If you head north into the Arctic Circle you can take in a bit of reindeer racing, at the same time keeping yourself warm by participating in one of the country's legendary vodka-drinking contests.

The jewel in Finland's sporting crown, however, remains the Sonkajarvi World Wife-Carrying Championships.

Originating in the 19th century when, apparently, it was common practice for men to steal wives from neighbouring villages, the contest involves husbands carrying their wives over a 253.5-metre (277-yard) obstacle course, cheered on by 7,000 ecstatic spectators.

The winner receives his spouse's weight in beer, and, more importantly, the honour of being Wife Carrying Champion for a year. Such things can mean a lot to a man.

Ugliest shapes

The United Kingdom, too, boasts a wealth of exciting sporting events. Forget Wimbledon and the F.A. Cup - if it is real drama you're looking for check out the Chipping Pig-throwing contest, or the Llanwrtyd World Bog Snorkelling Championships (in which, as the name suggests, competitors snorkel 60 yards through a peat bog, the winner being the one who does it the quickest).

Cumbria's Egremont Crab Fair is home to the World Gurning Championships - gurning being the art of crumpling your face into the ugliest shape possible - while the fact that they wear funny hats and ribbons does nothing to dispel the sense of rivalry among the competitors at the annual Walton Hall Morris Dancing Contest.

And let us not forget the now world-famous Cooper's Hill Cheese Rolling Contest where contestants chase a giant 7lb (3.2kg) Double Gloucester cheese down a hill, many of them falling over themselves and ending up in hospital as a consequence.

Elsewhere in Europe you can see - and take part in - the Munich Festival Beer Drinking Challenge (Germany), the Odalengo Truffle Hunting Competition (Italy), the Kiruna Snowball-Throwing contest (Sweden) and even the Trie-sur-Baise Pig -Screaming Championship (France).

These gems of sporting excellence may not get as much coverage as, say, the Barcelona Olympics did, but that should in no way detract from the skills they require nor the tension they are capable of generating.

A last-minute World Cup penalty shoot-out might get your adrenalin pumping. In terms of sheer edge-of-the-seat excitement, however, there are few things that can compete with a group of grown men fighting to catch-hold of a lard-covered piglet.

Stop your timers?

How did you do? The word count of this piece is 719 words. Calculate your score and add it to the chart at the end of the chapter.

 And comprehension? Answer these questions to find out:

1   Where did the World Screaming Championships take place?

    a   Geneva
    b   Godalming
    c   Goldap
    d   Guatemala

2   Name two countries that contestants came from.

    a   Japan and Austria
    b   China and Germany
    c   USA and Hungary
    d   Australia and France

3 What was special about Pawel Dabrowski's 125.3 decibels?

    a   It won the competition
    b   It was a world record
    c   It was a career best
    d   It broke a glass window

4 What occupation did the winner of the Screaming Championships have?

    a   Engineer
    b   Opera singer
    c   Teacher
    d   Housewife

5 How many mosquitoes did Henri Pellonpaa kill?

    a   20
    b   21
    c   22
    d   23

6 Where did the Wife-Carrying Championships take place?

    a   Singapore
    b   Sonkajarvi
    c   Stockholm
    d   Siberia

7 What did the World Wife-Carrying Champion receive?

    a   His wife's weight in beer
    b   A crate of beer
    c   His wife's weight in wine
    d   A tankard

8 How far do competitors snorkel in the peat bog?

    a   60 metres
    b   60 kilometres
    c   60 yards
    d   60 feet

9 What is gurning?

    a   Wearing funny hats and ribbons
    b   A type of Morris dancing
    c   Making grotesque faces
    d   Making clay models

10 Where does cheese rolling take place?

a   Keeper's Hill
b   Cooper's Hill
c   Carter's Hill
d   Camper's Hill

Mark your score on the graph at the end of the chapter.

If your speed and comprehension consistently improved across the tests, congratulations. It requires considerable application as well as deft use of the techniques to make a significant improvement so quickly.

If you found that you didn't always improve don't worry. Many people need a lot of practice before they see significant gains and sometimes comprehension gets worse before it gets better. Keep at it and both your speed and understanding will improve.

Trouble shooter

Here are some common problems people have had in workouts and some suggestions of how to deal with them.

Trouble	Solution
I start worrying about whether I'm going to remember anything and so lose track of what I'm reading.	This is one of the big challenges of learning to speed read. Whilst we're reading we start to wonder whether it's working. In the time that we're doing our wondering we've moved on five sentences and have lost the gist of the piece. We then worry about that and before we know it three paragraphs have gone. Trust yourself - if you feel yourself starting to worry refocus on what you're reading. Don't try to silence your internal voice, just redirect your attention.

Trouble	Solution
I move my pointer too fast for my eyes to keep up	Your pointer should be moving fast enough so that you should notice your eyes moving quickly, but not so fast that the text becomes blurred. Simply slow down.
My comprehension has dropped	This may be part of the learning process, although often this is a symptom of some other trouble. Look through the other troubles to see which may be the cause.
I can still hear a voice in my head	Removing subvocalisation can be a big challenge, particularly if you've always read that way. The best way to overcome this is to speed up to the point at which subvocalisations are no longer possible. Move your pointer a little faster.
I find it hard to focus	Are you free from distractions? Find a place where you can concentrate on the task at hand. It may also be that you're trying too hard. Don't see doing this as a pass or fail exercise but as learning a new skill.
I find it hard to use the pointer and fixate on a number of words at the same time	At first the idea of having larger fixations and using a pointer can seem incongruous. Think of the pointer as a metronome, keeping you to a steady pace, with the fixations as pulses of attention.

Reading without reading

'You must read this book,' your friend assures you. You don't want to, but you don't want to let them down either. Reading it quickly, using the earlier techniques, is an option but, quite honestly, even that is going to take too long.

There is a form of intelligent reading that is designed for exactly this need: when we want to devour a report, newspaper article, magazine or book, without actually reading it.

Its focus is on becoming mindful of our reading and it consists of six steps: prime, peek, peruse, participate, prudent, post mortem.

1 Prime

Before you even pick the book up, consider what you want from it and what you already know about the subject.

If we prime our thinking with some questions we are much more likely to find what we are looking for quickly. Some good priming questions are:

- Why am I reading this?

- What do I want to discover from it?

- What do I know about the subject?

- What do I know about the author?

Imagine you were introduced to a buffet for the first time and you thought you had to eat everything: that would be pretty daunting.

It's much the same with factual text. However, when we see the material as a source of information rather than something we must read from beginning to end, we can find what we want a lot faster.

2 Peek

This step is about searching for clues as to the whereabouts of the information and insights that we are after. Much reading time is spent churning through irrelevant material and peeking is designed so that we can cut this out.

Our cursory peek might include finding out whether there is:

- a table of contents, footnotes, an index, an index of tables

- headings and subheadings

- introductions and conclusions

As well as:

- how the book is arranged

- what the blurb on the front and back claims

At this stage we are getting familiar with the structure of the material but not the content. A 300-page book should take us about 5 minutes to peek at. Along the way we should highlight the areas we reckon are going to be useful to us, so that we can come back to them later. And if we don't think the material is going to give us what we want, then let's put it to one side and save ourselves a lot of bother.

3 Peruse

This is when we consider the style of the book and begin to get a sense of the content. It also starts the search for the core themes. Some books make this startlingly clear from the outset but, more often, the author wants us to read their whole work and so we will need to do some more investigating.

We do this by flicking through every page, at a rate of about a page per second. This might take another 5 minutes. As we are doing this we ask ourselves the following questions:

- What is the style of the book like?

- Are there key words or concepts which keep coming up?

- Are the sections highlighted at the peek stage the right ones?

- Is there any technical terminology? Where is it?

4 Participate

Now is the time for real reading, though even at this stage we don't want to waste our time on every word. It is the largest part of the reading process and one where the techniques in the earlier part of this chapter can be helpful.

Here we read the first and last sentence of every paragraph and possibly the first and last paragraph of those chapters that we identified as useful in our our initial scan. We consider what the authors are saying and what their key points are. This phase may take 30 minutes for a 300-page book.

Again we mark up the areas which are most relevant and discard those areas that do not fit with our purpose.

5 Prudent

The penultimate stage is prudent reading. Having marked those areas which contain the items which are of interest to us, we can now speed-read them. Ideally, this is done in 20-minute chunks with time for a stretch or change of atmosphere at the end of each section.

6 Post mortem

This final part of the process looks at how the reading was done, rather than the content of the book. What worked, what helped and where was time or comprehension lost? The first few attempts with the 6 Ps are going to be difficult but if we reflect on where the tools worked and where we had problems, then we will soon master the technique and devour documents in moments.

That'll impress them.

Tips from the pros

Here are some other techniques that increase the rate at which we get through a book.

Scanning

We all skim naturally, whether it be looking for a name in the phone book, running our eyes down the results page in Google, or checking the shopping list. We know what we're looking for, we just want to find it quickly. Scanning is particularly useful in the Peek step of the 6 Ps.

Skimming

Skimming is the process of passing our eyes across a page, picking out core bits of information and getting an overall impression of the text. Technically, we're not reading every word, but we can get the gist of the piece. When people report reading speeds of more than 600 words per minute the main technique they are using is skimming. You might use skimming in the Peruse step of the 6 Ps.

Superfluous paragraphs

One workout participant at the end of the first exercise had a reading speed of 600 words per minute which is significantly above average. She said that her reading speed was high because she missed out descriptions. She said that they rarely added to the narrative and so could be skipped altogether. If we find paragraphs that seem to be going nowhere, simply skip them.

Speed and comprehension chart

Write in your scores at the bottom of the chart and plot the points on the grid.

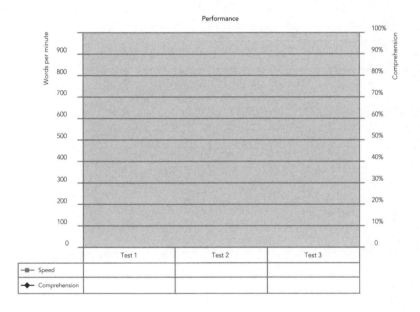

Performance

	Test 1	Test 2	Test 3
Speed			
Comprehension			

Answers to comprehension questions

Test 1	Test 2	Test 3
1 c	1 b	1 c
2 b	2 c	2 a
3 a	3 d	3 c
4 b	4 a	4 d
5 a	5 b	5 b
6 d	6 a	6 b
7 c	7 d	7 a
8 c	8 c	8 c
9 a	9 b	9 c
10 b	10 d	10 b

People power

People power can topple governments, create icons, make trends and change the way of the world. Closer to home, it is also one of the most resourceful ways to get more done in less time.

This section is filled with techniques to channel the power of the people around us so that we get more time to do what we want.

First up, the dream of so many flip-chart weary executives: Q, Fleeting meetings. Next, to provide ways to get other people to do brilliantly what we haven't got time to do at all: R, Off load. Then how to find a slot in a diary without windows, S, Getting time with time poor people. And to conclude, something that will improve our environment, T, Toxic time cultures.

If we apply these techniques sensitively, it won't just be us who gains but all the people around us: a source of time saving energy that will never run out.

Ⓠ Fleeting meetings

When it comes to time, are meetings the good guys? Or do they just pretend to be? People make out that meetings are going to save us time, but all too often it feels like they're devouring it with little to show in return.

Search for the hero

If a meeting were a hero of the time generating world, what kind of get together would it be?

Probably one that hasn't overrun too far and in which a few good decisions get made; one where results are achieved in a reasonable amount of time and everyone gets on famously. A meeting like that would certainly be considered a good use of time. But the quality of the time spent together is only one measure of time efficiency. Its real value will be felt later when it delivers long term gains in terms of time saved and impact made.

A meeting that is a great time generator is likely to

- result in decisions that are implemented swiftly

- anticipate key challenges so that pre-emptive action is taken

- get people so fired up that they are still buzzing weeks and months later

- strengthen relationships so that when problems occur, they can be solved quickly and amicably

- generate coalitions that can withstand resistance and promote their cause consistently

- build the skills and confidence of those involved

- create a shared understanding that enables those who were present to make the right judgements later, when they are alone

All that and, no doubt, much more.

More than a meeting

The new product division of a major manufacturer held a series of annual meetings to present their results. Employees would file into the lecture theatre in groups of 300 to hear the boss talk about the major achievements of the last 12 months and the challenges facing them in the next 12. A few people would ask questions and then everyone would leave.

A newly appointed Managing Director wanted to try something different. He was keen to show that he appreciated how hard everyone had worked during the year and also to give everyone the chance to realise the full extent of their achievements.

Working late into the night before, he and a few helpers lined the corridors with an exhibition illustrating all the triumphs and achievements of the past year. When people arrived for work they were directed through the exhibition. At the end were two massive white walls. On one, people were invited to write their feelings about the last year and on the other their hopes and fears for the year ahead.

As they left the exhibition they met the MD who thanked each of them individually and told them to go home and take the rest of the day off as they deserved it.

The mood was surprised and delighted. And the massive white walls with everyone's comments lasted for many months into the new year as a symbol of their collective enthusiasm.

Farewell to flabby meetings

Every meeting, be it a group of housemates planning a painting weekend, a theatre company preparing their next season, or a multi-national discussing a new product launch, has the potential to be a howling great waste of time. On the other hand, it could inform, inspire and invigorate, generating imaginative and far reaching decisions for some days, weeks or even years.

Trouble is, it's hard to know which kind of meeting you are in for.

The key lies in planning. And not just planning who will be there and what will be discussed; the key to a good, time generating meeting, is how. What business manuals call the 'Process'. It is in considering this process that we have the opportunity to create a meeting that will repay the time spent on it with interest. And that is what the rest of this chapter is about.

Purely the process

There are two elements to the process for a meeting:

- those things that need to be considered in advance: whom to invite, what to include on the agenda, and where to hold the meeting
- the action of the meeting: how long we spend on each subject, the order in which people speak, and so on

Part 1 - Setting the stage

Let's assume that this is 'your' meeting. You've called it, or you've been given the job of organising it. To ensure that you have covered everything, ask yourself the following five questions. You won't need all five on every occasion and they will have different weights for different kinds of get together, so feel free to pick and mix.

1 Why?
Cut to the chase by clarifying what you want to achieve. Is this meeting aiming to:

- inform
- generate ideas and discussion
- make a decision?

It may be all three, or only one or two. And the purpose may be different for each subject area under discussion. We may, for example, want to inform on progress of the planning application for the new cricket pavilion, gather ideas for raising funds to pay for it, and make a decision about how to project manage the building works.

2 Who?

Give careful thought to the guest list. Are the usual suspects the right people to invite, or would some new blood change the dynamic and bring a fresh perspective?

One Marketing Director asked the rest of his Board what they thought their potential customers were thinking and feeling. Each Director talked at length about what they imagined their potential customers wanted even though none of them actually fitted the demographic themselves.

Next, the Marketing Director brought into the meeting four individuals who had nothing to do with the company, each representing different elements of the target constituency. In turn, these guests gave their views about their likes, concerns and what they'd want from a company like this - views that were entirely different from what the Board Directors had imagined.

In this vivid example of 'showing rather than telling' the Marketing Director skilfully demonstrated that the management group didn't understand their customers simply by inviting the right people to the meeting.

3 Where?

Surroundings can have a big influence on how we think. The members of a London media company inspired themselves to think big by holding their meetings in tall buildings around London: Tate Modern, the London Eye, even the whispering gallery in St Paul's Cathedral.

If you get stuck for a suitable location, try thinking of it less as a meeting and more as a gathering, a get together, an assembly, a forum - a party, even. The word symposium, which is often used to describe a meeting where papers are presented, originally meant 'a drinking party or a convivial discussion'. They were very popular after banquets in Ancient Greece, apparently.

Approach the preparation in this spirit and you may find yourself with more than a flask of sour coffee and some flaccid sandwiches on the 3rd floor.

4   What?

At the heart of a great agenda lies clarity.

Clarity about content

A good agenda item makes it clear what it is about. An excellent item also explains what kind of outcome is wanted.

So, instead of:

- overseas

Which is pithy but a touch mysterious; try:

- where to launch outside the home territory
- desired result: a short list of countries to investigate

Clarity about procedure

If we know in advance how each subject is going to be discussed, we'll save a lot of time on the day.

'The opposite of talking isn't listening. The opposite of talking is waiting,' observed the American writer Fran Leibowitz. People are generally happier when they are talking and being listened to, so it pays to build in time for chat. Breaking into smaller groups helps even more as it means that several people can talk at the same time (without a battle).

Clarity on the order of discussion

10 ways to talk

1   Each person to give their views for one minute without interruption from anyone else.

2   Pros and Cons. The group discusses all the advantages of an idea before moving on to the disadvantages.

3   Break into pairs or small groups to discuss an issue and then return to share main insights.

4   Everyone to spend 30 seconds writing down their ideas first and then share. This helps encourage the quieter people to contribute.

5   Swap positions and ask each person to make the case for a view that is different to the one they hold.

6   Collective build, where each person writes down their idea and then passes it on for the next person to add to it and so on until each idea has gone full circle.

7   Posters on the walls with information; people go and read them and add their questions on Post-It notes which they stick on the relevant place.

8   Forcefield analysis. First we discuss all the things that are likely to get in the way or stop something happening. Next, all the things that will help it to happen.

9   Brainwriting. Individually, we write all our ideas or suggestions for a specific question on separate Post-It notes. We stick them on the wall. Then, together, we group them by theme.

10 A formal debate with a proposer and a seconder for and against the motion. Or a balloon debate where the least popular idea gets ditched at each round.

Imagine that you are the least informed person who will be at the meeting. Can you contribute to each item without needing information from discussions that are further down the agenda?

If there is no natural sequence, then start with the most important. This way an over-run early on is less serious.

Clarity about the time limits

Include an estimate for how long will be spent on each subject. It doesn't matter if you don't stick to it but if everyone is aware when a conversation is overrunning someone may suggest that it's time to move on.

Meetings without a chair

To keep meetings short, try removing the chairs. One well known company agreed on its new name in ten minutes. The reason: everyone wanted to get on with it so they could go back to their desks and sit down.

An advertising agency in London has different kinds of rooms for different kinds of meeting: some have stools for perching, others simply have a bar to lean on, one isn't a room at all, but a space in the middle of the corridor. Only one has chairs (and they're hard).

The sociologist Allen Bluedorn conducted an experiment in which 555 students were randomly assigned into groups of five. All of them would go into a meeting room to solve the same problem, one that demanded at least moderate amounts of creativity and judgement and where their success could be measured quantitatively. For half of them there was no furniture in the room, whilst for the other half there were five chairs and a table.

The quality of the results was statistically identical for the 56 groups who had stand up meetings as the 55 who sat down. However, the sit down meetings took, on average, 34% longer.

Making everyone stand up isn't the only way of keeping meetings crisp.

When British Cabinet meetings introduced a no smoking rule, the smokers became much more willing to compromise in meetings. There is also no coffee or biscuits in Cabinet meetings, which encourages the caffeine consumers and the grazers, which is pretty much everyone else, to remain sharp and to the point.

5 Who's my support?

Sometimes it is good to fly solo. Often, it is better to get some air cover. As one of the most effective ways of keeping control in a difficult meeting is to be in charge of the process, support on how the meeting is run is extremely valuable.

One way to do this is to share the draft agenda and ask for feedback from a couple of people who are coming to the meeting. Make sure they know that you want feedback on the agenda itself, not their views on each of the individual points.

One workout participant recalled interviewing each person before a particularly tricky meeting.

'There was a lot of tension on this subject and I wanted to discover each person's perspective first. This was extremely helpful. First, I was able to find some areas of common ground that, given the characters involved, would have been all but impossible to do if they'd first shared their views in the same room. I could therefore start the meeting with 'what we agree on' which got us off on a constructive footing. Secondly, once I knew where they were coming from I designed an agenda so that everyone's prime concern was covered at some stage, and they could see that. Thirdly, and most helpfully, it gave me a chance to build a relationship with each of them. This meant that they let me run the meeting rather than each trying to hijack it which is what, I gather, had happened when they'd got together in the past.'

On the pill

A manager in a pharmaceuticals company sent out what looked like a box of pills.

On the outside was written 'If there was a pill that guaranteed you'd come up with a brilliant new product idea, would you take it?' Inside, amongst the fake pills that were actually chocolates, there was a slip of paper that said: 'Unfortunately, the pill hasn't been invented yet but we can offer the next best thing, a brainstorm with many of the company's finest creative minds. Can you be tempted?'

Not only did everyone accept but they all turned up buzzing with energy and ideas prompted by this unorthodox invitation.

Part 2 - Taking the reins

Even the most assiduous preparation is no guarantee against time slipping away as discussions meander and participants bicker and bore.

To keep meetings on track there is one rule: govern the process.

To do this effectively you may choose to limit your own contributions to the discussion. The risk, otherwise, is that your role may be unclear and so you dilute your authority. Also, if you contribute heavily to both the content and the process, you are more likely to dominate the meeting which may damage the dynamic (depending, of course, on what you want to achieve).

With judicious use of questions and other techniques you can often make sure that your views are heard even if you aren't the one expressing them. And if you are the only person in the group with relevant, expert knowledge then the others will be only too keen for your contribution.

So the answer isn't abstinence, more like self-control.

You may even want to point out when you are giving your views as opposed to managing the process of the meeting: 'on this subject I have something I'd like to add to the debate'.

Here are 3 ways that you can control the process once the meeting is under way.

1 Keep on track

Start out by reminding people of the purpose of the meeting (ideally, written at the top of the agenda) and the journey you have in mind.

Ask if there are any questions about the process. There rarely are but this isn't the point. To keep authority the governor needs the approval of the people. If they agreed to your process at the outset it will be harder for them to hijack it later. You will also have created a consensus at the outset which gets things off to a positive start if you're about to enter a heated debate.

Now the structure of the meeting has been agreed, it can be a useful tool to keep the chat on track.

- If the meeting goes off on a tangent, ask, 'How does this fit with the South African strategy?' If it doesn't fit with the current sub- ject on your agenda, it can be written down somewhere as a subject for later, if there's time, and you can steer the discussion back on course.

- If time is running out, say so: 'We have used up the 30 minutes we allocated to this.'

Then the choice is between making a decision: 'We will now move on'; and asking the group what they want: 'Do we want to continue on this? If so, for how long and what will we lose from the rest of the agenda?' The advantage of asking the group is that they will then support the decision.

If someone challenges the process, remember this is where you draw much of your meeting authority from. Agree to alter it only if you are confident that it will improve the experience.

A consultant recalled running a workshop with a group of bankers who were prospective clients. The two most senior bankers hogged the conversation, vehemently disagreeing with each other on everything. When the consultant suggested that they split into two groups, as the agenda suggested, they flatly refused. On this, for the first time that day, they were united.

The consultant asked again. Again they refused, saying that they found the current conversation just fine. The consultant believed that they were enjoying arguing with each other but that nothing useful would come out of the workshop if they continued in this way.

'In your meetings you can do what you like. I called this meeting and I am happy for you to share whatever views you have but one thing I am asking is that, as we agreed at the outset, you separate into two groups for forty minutes and then we can come back and talk more together.' He paused, and then added in a way that sounded as much like an order as a request, 'Please.'

The two bankers looked a little put out but realising that the consultant wasn't going to back down, reluctantly agreed with a shrug that suggested 'if you care that much, then fine; it doesn't really matter'.

But it did. The break not only transformed the dynamic and enabled the other people to contribute to the debate but also, by separating the two antagonists, made the discussion when the full group resumed much more constructive.

The consultant went on to advise this organisation for several years. He puts down as one of the turning points that secured this relationship the moment he stood firm on the process for the workshop.

2 Stimulate participation

The governor of the meeting is responsible for making sure that everyone gets enough air time. But not too much. Once again, managing the process is the way to do this.

Silent member

First, spot them. It's easy to be distracted by those who are making all the noise but wise to identify who isn't taking part. They may have a brilliant idea or be preparing to ambush the debate - whatever is going on in their head it's good to get it out.

'I try to get everyone to have said something within the first half hour,' explained a workout participant and meeting maestro. 'I ask them straightforward questions but ones that require more than 'yes' or 'no' answers. Anything from 'what would you like to get out of this meeting?' to 'what do you agree with most out of what you've heard so far?'

Chatterbox

They may not draw breath but somehow you will need to interrupt: 'just to make sure I've understood what you're saying'. Summarise what they've said and check they agree with our version. Thank them for their insights and then turn to someone else.

Know it all

However much of an expert they think they are, you will need to stop them. As with the chatterbox, summarise their views and check they agree with your version. Then ask if there are any other views. If the know-it-all tries to interrupt be firm, 'You've given your views and you can come back again later but let's just hear what Carole has to say.' Of course, we need to make sure that we do go back to them later, but by that stage they've probably forgotten what they were going to say or may have changed their mind having listened to all the other arguments.

Again, all we are doing is managing the discussion. We don't need to agree or disagree with them; someone else will do that for us.

3 Take out the tension

Sometimes a meeting can get nasty. Once more, managing the process is the best way to defuse the tempers.

Sabotage

A young workout participant from a utility company recalled being sent round his company to gather views from employees. All had gone well in the first seven discussion groups but when it got to the eighth, with a selection of meter readers, he ran into difficulties.

'We've got nothing to say to you, sonny boy. We've been around long enough and they never listen to us. What's the point in wasting our breath?'

The young man tried to get them to change their mind as hard as he could. He promised that this time their views really would be heard; he committed that he, personally, would deliver them to the Managing Director; he told them how the other groups had come up with lots of great ideas. It made no difference. The men sat cross armed and defiant.

'It's a shame. I'll just have to go back with the views of seven groups,' the youth from central office concluded, and he started to pack up.

'Hey, not so fast young man,' protested the leader of the group, *'you seem like a fine enough lad, we don't want to send you back empty-handed. We'll talk to you, won't we boys?'* And they did.

Given the choice between exclusion and participation most will opt for the latter. And if they don't, you don't want them there.

Anger management

Matt stood up and to one side of his chair. 'Are you angry with me or are you angry with this chair?' he asked the other people in the meeting. Suddenly, the extreme tension evaporated as everyone laughed. 'We're just angry. It's not your fault, Matt, or the chair's', one of them explained, 'sorry if we were shouting at you, it's nothing personal.'

If Matt had been contributing to the content of the discussion he wouldn't have got away with this. But because he was strictly concerned with the process, he could point out what was going on and, even better, in a way that broke the mood.

Seeking consensus

Who wants a consensus? Unless it is in everyone's interests to get agreement it's going to be difficult to find one, so it's worth checking. And if they say they do, ask what they see as the consequences of failing to reach a decision. If not getting a conclusion on the budget means they can't spend any money and will have to postpone their favourite project, this is very different from simply having to meet again in a week's time.

Once the appetite to get to an agreement has been established, then it is time to explore each person's position to discover what their true interests are.

We all want the desk by the window. This is our position. And it looks irreconcilable. But our interests, that is, the reasons we want the desk by the window, may be different. Richard wants natural light; Sue sees it as a sign of importance; Dan reckons it's quieter there; and Sam wants to be able to see her new car as she's worried it might get stolen.

Once we know everyone's interests, it is easy to find a solution. Sue gets a desk next to the directors, Dan in the corner with the least traffic and Sam has a webcam trained on her pride and joy.

Intransigence

If someone won't budge at all, ask them 'what is the one thing that would convince you to change your mind?' If they say 'nothing' then you might as well pack your bags. More likely, they will come up with something, however extreme. This gets them to accept that they could, at least in theory, alter their view. We have movement.

One thought on meetings. Only one.

Master the process and you will master the meeting. Time benefits galore.

In the thick of it

Stuck in a meeting that's going nowhere? Many of the techniques outlined elsewhere can be used by a member of the meeting as much as by the person ostensibly in charge. Just, it requires a little more sensitivity.

A workout participant, Ghita, recalled being in a meeting about launching a new prize for young people in film. She was the only person in the room who didn't work in the film industry so, for a while, she just listened. After a while it became clear that the discussion was going round in circles with each person eager to give their views, and talk about their achievements, but no direction to the discussion and no progress. The person who was supposed to be running the meeting would chip in with the odd anecdote and opinion but wasn't doing anything to steer the conversation.

At last, she spoke. 'I'm new to this,' she apologised, 'and I'm thoroughly enjoying listening to all your stories,' she flattered, 'but I'm wondering if we are on the right track for deciding how this prize could work. I may have got this wrong but it seems to me that there are five questions that we need to answer and that if we discuss each of them in turn, we will end with a clear idea of what the prize will look like. Would it be worth me sharing what I think these questions are?'

The rest of the group realised that the conversation, however enjoyable, wasn't going anywhere and were willing to listen. They then used the five questions to organise the rest of the meeting. And each time the conversation looked like it was going off track, someone would say, 'I'm not sure this is answering Ghita's questions.'

Even though Ghita knew less about film than anyone else, she became the heroine of the meeting.

If a meeting is proving a waste of time then everyone will be grateful if you can put them out of their misery, so long as you do it delicately.

(R) Off load

If we could off load some of the things we have to do to someone else it would save us time. Yet many of us find handing over tasks extremely precarious. We may not trust the person who would be taking them on, or we may feel so emotionally attached to the activity that it's agony to let it go. Whatever our reason, however, the root of the problem usually lies in how we delegate.

A cautionary tale

Richard had agreed to housesit for his parents whilst they were away on holiday. As well as feeding the cat, his father had asked him if he would plant some new trees in the garden. Richard, a committed city dweller to whom country living was something of a mystery, agreed cautiously. Cats he could handle, but trees? Don't they have roots and things? Fortunately, his father made things easy. He sent a diagram showing exactly where the trees should go. He also sent details of the kind of tree he wanted, the address of the nursery where they could be bought, a cheque for the right amount of money, and a detailed schedule for daily watering. Reassured, Richard got on with the job and followed his father's instructions to the letter. The saplings were bought, paid for and planted, exactly as his father had instructed. And they were watered, for 10 minutes each every day, as his father had stipulated.

When his father next called, Richard recounted his success.

'*And you put in some fresh soil, didn't you?*' asked his father.

Fresh soil?

Richard scrabbled in the waste bin and retrieved the piece of paper with his father's instructions. 'You didn't say anything about adding fresh soil.'

'I didn't think I needed to. I mean, how can a young tree grow in earth that is full of stones? Really, I should have waited and done it myself.'

And so the story ends with a bad outcome for everyone. Richard feels hard done by, his father is disappointed, and as for the trees, well, last time Richard looked they weren't exactly flourishing.

So what went wrong?

Both sides had good intentions and the challenge wasn't beyond Richard's capability. He wasn't being stupid and his father did a good job in giving highly detailed instructions. So, was the job of planting new trees not suitable for delegation as his father concludes? Not at all.

The reason why the handover of tree planting from father to son failed lies in the manner in which the delegation was done.

Made to measure

A skilled delegator fits their delegation mode to the requirements of the job at hand. Is the aim to hand over the task permanently, or is this just a quick fix because we are too busy on this occasion? Must the task be completed in a prescribed way or is their room for the person taking it on to improvise?

Asking these kinds of question enables us to decide which method is most appropriate: Precision delegation, Capability delegation, or a mix of the two.

Precision delegation

In this kind of delegation the focus is on the task. When the handover is well done, the communication is specific, thorough and crystal clear. The instructions concentrate on the present and on the immediate future: what needs to be done, when, how, and by whom. Do you understand the instructions? OK, off you go and do it.

In precision delegation the person doing the delegating knows exactly what they want and the person being instructed has the job of simply getting on with it.

Please can you lay the table for supper? Here is one setting laid out just how I want it; all the others need to be the same. We also need salt and pepper, four mats for hot dishes, two at each end, and two jugs of water - use the glass ones in the end cupboard. If you run out of paper napkins, there is another packet in the bottom drawer.

The commander in the battlefield, the huddles in American football, the surgeon in the operating theatre, the film director organising a camera crew, the team leader briefing a temporary member of staff; these are all cases where precision delegation is the norm. And with good reason.

- It's quick.

- It's clear. There is little room for ambiguity or misinterpretation.

- It's a simple way to transfer knowledge from an expert to a novice.

- It can reduce risk. The person is likely to do what they have been asked and, as long as they've been asked to do the right things, all should go well.

- It keeps control with the person doing the delegation.

Precision delegation also has its drawbacks. The person taking on the task may cease using their initiative. In the story above, Richard's father used precision delegation and, as a result, his son simply obeyed instructions. If he'd thought about it, Richard would probably have realised that the trees need fresh soil. The point is that he didn't think - the precision delegation encouraged him to switch off and simply follow the orders.

Anyone who has ever had a bad experience assembling a piece of flat pack furniture will know about the down side of precision delegation. In an attempt to keep to the instructions - 'place upright A into the lateral groove in section B whilst rotating section C through the left hand opening in the underside of upright B' - we lose sight of the big picture, quite literally. Faced with a clear diagram and a few key pointers we might have been able to work it out for ourselves; confronted with these rigid commands our brain turns to mush.

There are other disadvantages to precision delegation:

- It can be unpleasant being on the receiving end. As a result, it can damage relationships rather than enhance them with the task being done grudgingly. If you want enthusiasm then this is not the way to get it.

- It doesn't build good will or skills in the long term. The individual on the receiving end is not going to be more able or more willing to take on tasks from you in the future. A busted flush.

- It doesn't invite any insights from the other person. If two heads are better than one, then this isn't getting the benefit of the second one. The other person could just as well be a sophisticated robot.

Given the rather large downside of this kind of delegation, it is always worth considering an alternative from the other end of the delegation spectrum.

Capability delegation

With capability delegation the focus is less on the task and more on the person who is taking it on. The intention is to equip them with the skills and insights to do the task themselves and take the initiative when faced with the unanticipated.

The scope of the instructions used in capability delegation is much broader, and there is more conversation. You may discuss why the task needs to be done in the first place, why the person taking it on is right for the job, different ways of approaching the challenge and how this particular task fits in with other activities. The goal is to engage the person and get them thinking.

So, to return to the example of laying the table for supper. Rather than spending time laying out a setting for the person to copy, we might simply ask them to use the same setting as last night, but point out the changes in the meal.

I've made soup tonight.

'OK, I'll put out soup spoons. Will you need side plates for bread?'

Yes, and the main course is salad.

'So no mats for hot dishes?'

That's right. And I thought we'd have white wine tonight, instead of red.

'I'll use the smaller glasses then. And some tumblers for water.'

Thanks.

'OK, I'll give it a go.'

When capability delegation is done well, the person who is handing over the activity talks less than the person who is taking it on. There are fewer instructions and more encouragement to ask questions and use initiative. The benefits for the person taking on the challenge are also made clear (it will show you as an original thinker, supportive friend, potential team leader, etc.).

By encouraging people to work things out for themselves the capability approach to delegation is helpful in many ways:

- It makes the task more enjoyable and engaging for the person taking it on.

- It increases the chances of a successful outcome when unpredictable things happen.

- It generates enthusiasm and discretionary effort as the person taking on the task is doing it for themselves as much as anyone else.

- It may mean you discover better solutions as the options are being discussed, not just at the beginning but also throughout, as the situation develops.

- It builds strong relationships. The person on the receiving end feels appreciated for their views and trusted to do the task well.

- It ensures that future delegation is quicker and successful. The person taking on the task is more confident and capable next time around.

Cure all

Delegation is the nearest thing that time-poor people get to a panacea. As we hand over more and more of what we don't want to do we are left with an increasing number of hours and days to devote to the things we really do enjoy.

Precision delegation works like a quick-acting painkiller. It hits the spot and relieves the current time pressure straight away but it won't prevent it coming back. Capability delegation is more like preventative medicine. It will ease the immediate problem a little but its main benefit is to give you more time in future. It is also the kind of delegation that will win you friends and supporters, which is a welcome side effect.

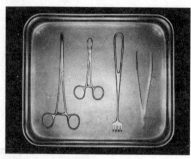

Precision, please

Using the delegation spectrum

Usually, the optimum strategy doesn't lie at either end of the spectrum, we have to move up and down it. However, this can take practice. It's a common mistake to start with a very precise handover, feel slightly guilty, dilute it with a half-hearted attempt at capability delegation, then be worried that it might go wrong and finish off with a warning or detailed instruction thinly disguised as advice. The person on the receiving end is left, at best, baffled and, more likely, deeply frustrated.

By contrast, the delegation maestro moves up and down the spectrum like a concert pianist. They draw from the different modes to create a melody.

For example: we might start with precision delegation on the outcome we want - 'We need to recruit someone to redesign the website. They have to be available to start at the end of the month.' Then we explain what's in it for the person taking over the task, if they deliver - 'You'll be working alongside the new designer. If you look after the recruitment you can make sure we find someone you feel comfortable with.'

Next, we shift towards more capability delegation on how to get there - 'It's important we find someone with experience in our area of publishing - what would be the best way to attract someone like that?'

Depending on how this has gone, we might decide to revert to the precision style of delegation, or leave them to get on with it, having agreed how and when to review progress.

Mastery of the delegation techniques takes practice but it is worth persevering. There isn't a template to follow; we need to make our own decisions on the way. Inevitably, we will make errors but so long as we learn from these, we will increasingly hand over assignments in a way that delivers the right results with minimum fuss and maximum appreciation. And think of all that extra time.

Delegation ready-reckoner

Here are some of the factors to help decide which end of the spectrum to head towards.

	Precision	Capability
Capability of the person	Low - they have minimal experience in this area	High - they have relevant experience or suitable skills
Complexity of the outcome	Low - I can easily explain what success looks like	High - a good outcome would involve a lot of different elements
Chances of needing to take the initiative	Low - it is already clear exactly what needs to be done	High - the outcome may be clear but the route to get there is not
Stake the person has in a successful outcome	Low - it won't make a great deal of difference to them either way	High - there are big gains for them if they get it right
Likelihood of future handover to the same person	Low - this is a one-off	High - I'd like to be able to hand over more things to them in future

If you think you won't succeed, you won't

Here are the most frequently cited delegation fears from work-out participants, and some suggestions for more helpful ways of approaching the task.

Normal fear	Healthy alternative
It'll be quicker if I do it myself	It might be this time, but it won't be next time or the time after
I can do it better	I can't do everything. 80% is good enough for this activity
I am frightened it will go wrong	We can agree on frequent updates so I can spot problems early on
I feel like I'm losing control	If I have to be in control all the time I won't have the time to do other things
It's urgent	Lots of things are urgent and I can't do them all without help
I'm not completely clear what needs to be done	When we talk it through we can make it clearer
I want it done my way	There might be a better way and we can agree in advance how to do the task, as well as what needs to be done
I don't trust them	I can start by delegating small tasks and see what happens
I don't know if it is my place to delegate	Anyone can delegate - it is simply an agreement between two people about who does what
I feel that the task is my responsibility	Handing over the task isn't the same as handing over responsibility
It's a bit unfair, dumping on someone else like this	They may enjoy this or see it as a chance to learn. Just because I don't want to do it doesn't mean that they won't
It went wrong last time	I can use this experience to increase the chances that it will go right this time

What's your contract?

The concept of precision and capability delegation was developed from research that examined the Psychological Contracts between individuals.

Described as Transactional or Relational, these contracts are the unwritten agreements that dictate our behaviour and expectations of others. Transactional contracts are similar to those that underlie precision delegation - they tend to be short term, clearly articulated and focused on a particular task or transaction. For example, when we employ a plumber, we expect him to arrive, walk from the front door to the kitchen, fix the washing machine and leave. Any other behaviour would be outside the terms of the contract.

A relational contract, on the other hand, is more open ended. Like capability delegation it is less prescribed and often involves considerable investment from both parties. Marriage is perhaps the ultimate relational contract.

Give your mind a workout

I TRY Next time someone tries to hand something over to you using precision delegation, use questions to turn it more towards capability delegation.

Here are some questions that may help.

- What would success look like for you?

- Why is this task important?

- Who or what else is depending on it?

- What are the skills that are most needed?

- Why do you want me to do it?

(S) Getting time with time poor people

Who's putting you on hold?

Elsewhere in this book there are plenty of suggestions about how to deal with people who want more of your time than we can give. But what happens when we're the one doing the asking; when it's our time that is being eaten up as hanging about waiting for a decision, a sign off, advice or attention?

This chapter shows how to step out of the waiting room and get time with people who don't particularly want to find a match for our unrequited time.

Because I'm worth your while

Even the busiest people will find time for something they consider important. However much they've got on if an hour with you will guarantee them a house in Malibu, a recording contract, or whatever is at the top of their list of desires, they will find that hour.

The trick to getting time with time poor people is to make them consider time with us as time well spent. There are various ways that we can do this.

First date

A journalist in New York was keen to get a story from the President of a prestigious bank. She wrote, she emailed, she called. Each time she left a message with his PA, she was assured that he would return her call but he never did.

One day she rang his office and asked to be put through to Bob.

'Who is it?'

'Just tell him it's his ex-wife.' A few clicks later and Bob comes on the line.

'Nancy?'

'Er, actually it's not, it's ...'

After Bob swore that it was the darndest, most low down trick he'd ever come across in business, he relented and gave the journalist the interview that she had been so desperately seeking.

When asked how she knew Bob had an ex-wife, she replied, 'I didn't, but given his age and status I reckoned the odds were on my side.'

We don't have to be quite this sneaky to get time with busy people, but knowing what matters to them will go a long way towards getting their attention in the first instance.

A senior director bemoaned the fact that, during the period when his company was about to be floated on the stock market, he received numerous unsolicited sales letters asking for meetings but not one of them referred to the imminent flotation. 'It was widely reported in all the papers and yet not one person even mentioned it or acknowledged the impact it was likely to have. If they had, I would probably have agreed to meet.'

Do the research to find out what makes them tick. If we understand their hopes, fears and dreams we can connect our request to their priorities. In this way we make the prospect of time spent with us far more attractive.

Through a friend

The best way to find out what is on someone's mind is to ask a friend (of theirs). This has two benefits: it is likely to give us up-to-date inside information and it means that we might be able to garner an introduction.

The introduction could be direct, when Richard introduces you to Judy, by email or over a drink. Or indirect, when we use the name of a mutual acquaintance as the reason to meet: John thought you would be the perfect person to talk to and suggested I get in touch.

A business school has an online game, which sets players the challenge of getting a meeting with the CEO. Unbeknown to the students, the trick lies in spotting who the influencers are further down the hierarchy and meeting with them first, so that you get introduced up the chain. If you go straight to the CEO you will get rebuffed and you will need to get more endorsements to get a meeting at the second attempt. The game works because it is not far off the reality.

If we can't hook our elusive person through a direct introduction or an indirect recommendation, then the next best route is to use the name of someone they respect.

Appeal to the ego

I read your book, heard you speak, went to your exhibition, saw the article about you in the papers. Few of us can resist the approach of an appreciative fan. All the better if they are a well informed one too.

Tell a professor that you've been studying Yeats and thought his insights on the later poems were amongst the most acute you've come across, and he's sure to read on. Explain that you were particularly intrigued by his comments on Yeats' interest in spiritualism and would like to include his conclusions in a paper you're researching, and he's already warming the pot for tea.

If you are a fashion student who wants to meet with a great designer, make sure they know that you were at their last three shows and have an opinion on why they were so innovative.

And if you don't have any direct experience to refer to, then resort to praise. Compliment them on achievements that reflect well on them as an individual, rather than praising a specific achievement. 'You have a reputation for caring about what customers think ...'

And if possible link it to the reason why you want their time. 'With your track record at turning engineering concepts into profitable businesses ...'

If you know they are particularly susceptible to fawning then gush away, otherwise keep it on a leash.

Close up and personal

If you want your message to stick, keep it concrete and make it personal.

Psychologist Adrian Furnham researched the common sources of errors in decision making. His results showed that concrete information (for example, vivid examples, personal anecdotes) make more of an impact than abstract information. So, if we are considering buying a new car, a friend's experience of a particular make (concrete information) is likely to carry more weight than a consumer report (abstract information) even if the report is written by a panel of experts.

This goes some way to explaining why a personal recommendation or introduction is likely to be more compelling to the person on the receiving end.

Make it attractive

After the first space tourist surely, soon, the first inter-galactic corporate entertainment: Big Boys Inc invites you to a walk on the moon. If that seems a little far fetched, the 'conferences' in Hawaii, the corporate tents in Monaco and the company boxes at Covent Garden all serve as abundant reminders that, if we want to get time with time poor people, it pays to make it appealing.

'You may not remember, but we had dinner a few years ago in New York. The restaurant has since disappeared but you have gone on to great things and so, in a rather different way, have we. I was wondering if you would like to join me for dinner again. It would be a great opportunity to catch up and share insights.'

This invitation appeals on several levels. First, the personal connection, then the flattery - the restaurant may have failed but they haven't - topped off with the lure of lunch. Make it a good restaurant in a fabulous location so that even if the meeting isn't a good use of time, it will be in pleasant surroundings.

It also pays to make it easy. 'No timescale, it could be lunch or dinner and I'll call your office to see if it appeals.' Remove all the blocks that you anticipate so all they have to do is agree to meet.

And if your elusive person isn't the corporate entertaining type? If they spend their spare time building dry stone walls for the National Trust? Well then, it's time to dig out your Wellington boots and get out the trowel …

The same principles can be applied to getting time with a teenager. When they appear to be fused to their computer and their bedroom door is plastered with signs that say 'musician at work - do not enter', you may imagine it's going to be difficult to get time with them. But buy concert tickets, or offer to drive them to a trade show for home composers, and you are more than likely to find that their time is your time.

Thought for food

In the 1930s, psychologist Gregory Razran became interested in the associations that we attach to food. Razran was interested in the work of Pavlov, who demonstrated that dogs will salivate at the sound of a bell if they have been trained to associate the bell with food.

Razran hypothesised that human beings associate likeability with food and would therefore feel good about messages that they experienced whilst eating. To test this he asked people to rate a series of political statements. Months later, when the subjects had forgotten about the statements, they were asked to rate them again. Comparing their responses he found that those statements that people rated over lunch received significantly higher approval ratings than those that were rated without food.

Persistence pays

Many of these techniques won't work first time, even when we combine them skilfully. Other factors may play a part; our request may arrive when the person is in a bad mood, or when they are preoccupied with a personal issue. A tight deadline may mean that they have blocked their diary to anyone except friends and colleagues. These aren't permanent states and the refusal wasn't personal - keep at it.

We need to talk

We can find ourselves repeatedly having to pursue the same person. Their input might be essential for a project to progress, or their sign off before a piece of work can move into production, but with bulging diaries these top dogs consider that their time is needed for other matters.

The trick lies in thinking about their interests and concerns and hook them with something that matters to them, not us. Point out what will happen if we don't get their attention - painting the picture in colours that will resonate.

If reputation is important to them, tell them that their sign off will prevent the company from missing a deadline and looking sloppy. If growing the business is their prime concern, point out that their input will help exceed client expectations.

What do bosses want?

London Business School regularly researches what the leaders of businesses in over 20 countries want from the people who work directly for them.

Over the past few decades, expectations have changed dramatically. The focus used to be on technical capability, specialist knowledge and, at a push, strategic thinking. Today, their top priorities are predominantly the soft areas of business: interpersonal skills (33%), getting real experience (17%), sharpening up their image (13%), acting like leaders (11%), talking to me (11%), and clarifying where they are going. There was only one 'hard' request in the top 10: provide accurate numbers (15%).

All of which helps if we're trying to get a slice of time with the big cheese.

Once you've got their attention, hit the ground running. Keep the request crisp and focused, providing information on a need to know basis only. If they only need to check part of a document, then print out the appropriate pages, don't expect them to wade through the whole thing.

If the other person feels that we appreciate their time pressure and are making an effort to use their time well, they will be inclined to find the time in future.

How well are you using my time?

It can feel like getting in the door is the only bit that matters. It isn't. If we want to see these people again, our chances of succeeding are going to depend on how well we use their time on this occasion.

The following tips will help ensure that the meeting is a good experience from their perspective.

Why are you here?

Keep the rapport building chat short and to the point. Explain why you've asked to see them (they've probably forgotten) and, ideally, sprinkle gently with light flattery.

'Last time you gave me some advice on how to handle production which I followed and we were able to launch two weeks early. This time I am coming to you for a decision. In particular, whether to roll out the customer programme, run a pilot or put it on hold for now.'

Busy people like to be given options - it saves them having to do too much thinking - but they also want their views to matter, so presenting a series of alternatives is usually a good thing.

If this is part of a larger process then it's well worth explaining how it fits in. 'This is the first of a series of conversations with each member of the Executive. I will share the findings and make a recommendation at your meeting on the twenty-first. Do you want to see the presentation before then?'

If the conversation is part of something larger, it makes their contribution feel more important. It's not just a conversation between the two of us; it is part of an important journey in which they are influencing both the direction and the outcome. Even better, their views are likely to reach a wider audience. And did you notice the sneaky invitation for another meeting? With time poor people, best to get in early.

Give 'em the beef

Deliver the essential information straight away but keep it to headlines, unless you know they have an appetite for detail. Give the content structure but, above all, keep it brief. They can always ask questions if they want to find out more.

Time to chat

Important people like to talk. Usually, quite a lot. Make sure that they have plenty of opportunity to share their views. We need to be careful that we don't take up all the allotted time expounding our own opinion. 70:30 in their favour is a good rule of chat.

When they get going, it's essential to demonstrate that we are listening avidly. This doesn't mean taking copious notes, but it does mean giving complete attention whilst they are speaking, asking relevant questions, challenging where necessary, and giving brief summaries along the way to check we've understood correctly.

Whilst we were trying to get their time, they held the power. Now we are in the conversation we are equals and we can act as such. That means sufficient respect to acknowledge that they matter and enough distance to show we keep our own counsel. A funny comment, a smile or even a laugh can help too. If the time spent with us is enjoyable as well as productive, our next request for their time is more likely to be granted.

'I always have a piece of information or an anecdote that I think they will find useful,' explained a particularly effective networker. 'If they feel that they have got something from our conversation they will usually be happy to meet me again.'

A crisp conclusion

If we agreed to spend a certain amount of time together then it is important that we don't overrun. If they are enjoying the conversation so much that they want to continue, then that's their call. We made a contract and if we want to build a reputation as someone who uses other people's time well, we need to stick to it.

Conclude the conversation with:

- a summary of the main points that they have made
- a decision on what happens next
- thanks

And that's all.

Give your mind a workout

I SPY Observe who you agree to see, when you have a choice.

- What techniques do they use to get access to your time?

- What do you feel about your time together?

- What do they do that encourages you to spend time with them again (or not)?

Noticing what works on us is a great way of building up a portfolio of tactics and techniques that we can adopt when we want to get time with other, time poor people.

I TRY Think of someone with whom you want to get some time and imagine you are them. Answer the following questions from their perspective, always starting with 'I ...' or 'My ...'. If you can't answer the question then move on but make a note - this is where to focus your research.

- What is your name?

- What is your occupation?

- What do you like about your job/role/work?

- What worries you?

- What is your priority at work for the next 3/6/12 months?

- What about life outside work. What are the highlights? and the lowlights?

- If there was one thing in your life that could be sorted, what would it be?

- Have you ever heard of/What do you think about [insert your real life name]?

- What would make it worth your while to see him/her?

Carry on generating your own questions. Keep going for as long as you can. The better you understand the person whose time you want the greater your chances of getting it.

(T) Toxic time cultures

Some people struggle with taking control of their time. They explain that they really have tried, they've used the tools, they learnt the techniques, they've done the exercises, but still they don't get the results they want. 'It's not my fault,' they say, frustrated. And they are right - it isn't their fault. Sometimes the problem is bigger than us - sometimes the problem is in the culture.

When we are in a group or an organisation that has a toxic time culture we can't help but pick up bad habits. Often we don't even know that we are doing it and, as a result, we may give ourselves a tough time for something that isn't our fault.

Once we identify the time culture that we are operating in, we can begin to understand the impact it has, not only on us, but on those around us. If we can spot the unwritten rules we can learn how to operate within them, to our advantage. We can also find ways to challenge and change them.

Transforming a culture may sound like a tall order, but even one small cog has more power than it thinks.

Don't touch the bananas

Picture five monkeys in a room. In the corner, there is a chair and, hanging over the chair, a bunch of bananas. Being monkeys they head straight for the chair but instead of getting a free banana, they get an icy cold shower of water, triggered by the experimenters in the next room. Surprised and probably a little put out, the monkeys nevertheless get the point. Keep away from the corner and forget about the bananas.

At this point the experimenters remove one monkey from the group and introduce another one. The remaining four monkeys watch as their new companion makes for the corner of the room and then, knowing what's coming next, they beat him up to stop him getting to the chair. As a learning experience it's pretty effective. The new monkey decides that he'll do without the banana.

The experimenters continue to remove and replace the monkeys and the same scene is played out over and over again. Finally, there are no monkeys left who have seen the original drenching but that doesn't matter; the corner has now become a no-go zone. Avoiding the corner is now a rule of the group and everyone abides by it. Maybe one day a particularly presumptuous monkey will get around to asking why this rule exists. If he does he'll probably receive an answer that goes something like this:

'It's how we do things here.'

In other words, it's our culture.

The rules of house

Unwritten rules, unspoken attitudes, history, stories, values, traditions, beliefs, jokes, language, styles of dress and ways of speaking - all this and much more creates the culture of a group. Be it a family, a tennis club or a multinational, rules and conventions evolve. Countries have cultures, nationalities have cultures, families have cultures. Most of us move between a number of different cultures in the course of our daily lives. They provide the framework within which we act, and, as we saw with the monkeys, they can exert considerable impact on our behaviour. Some cultures fit us well: others feel less comfortable. One element of a culture that can help us or hinder us is its attitude to time.

The leadership often sets time mood. Clinton's White House was famously 15 minutes late for everything. Age also makes a difference: amongst British twentysomethings lateness is not considered a big deal. In a survey most of them said they wouldn't call ahead, even if they were running an hour late, whereas 82% of those over 50 claimed they were never late for anything.

But often there is no discernible cause - attitudes to time are simply endemic within an organisation. The Mind Gym workouts are run in a vast range of organisations. Typically, the actual start time differs from the published start time most acutely in those companies with the highest paid people: investment banks and management consultancies. By contrast, high street retailers and public sector organisations tend to kick off on the dot. It's hard to put these variations down to the whims of management. It's too consistent within industries and professions for that.

Doing the done thing

Some attitudes to time can be extremely helpful. The armed services have a consistent approach that aids discipline and makes it easier for different countries to work together; deadlines are an immutable force that drives journalists to get their keys on the keyboard and produce the copy.

Equally, time cultures can evolve that are destructive, not only for individuals but for the group as a whole. Like the monkey's warning to their companions, most of these practices start off with the best intentions but mutate into something rather less benign. Take, for example, long hours. Sometimes a project demands we put in the effort and go the extra mile. It's when extra long days become unofficial, non-negotiable, company policy that the alarm needs to be sounded.

Greg, a workout participant who worked in a financial services company, described how putting in 'face time' was considered essential in his office. Everyone felt they had to be seen to be there first thing in the morning and late into the evening, even when they had nothing to do. Greg's strategy was to leave an empty jacket on his chair and to set his computer to wake up at 8 a.m. when it would send off a bunch of pre-prepared emails and launch a program that changed the graph on his screen every 15 minutes. Greg would arrive in person sometime around 10 a.m. Fiendishly clever but even Greg agreed it wasn't the best use of his problem solving skills.

Good time gone bad

There are a number of ways in which a benign practice can become time destructive. The most common symptoms sound like this:

'I spend all my time in meetings'
'Another working party'

'I can never get on with my own work'
'Long hours and getting longer'

All these statements express a symptom of an unhealthy attitude towards time. The good news is that they can be changed. And the person who can make those changes happen is, well, you.

This may sound a bit unrealistic. David and Goliath is one thing but trying to reform an entrenched time culture that has built up over years, maybe decades, is quite another. The first thing to realise is that we can always do something. Just because we don't have a seat in the boardroom doesn't mean we can't make change happen. The little guy has plenty of power, if he/she chooses to use it skilfully.

It is not going to happen overnight and we can't do it alone. It will require coalitions, or groups of like-minded people. But these are things we can create. If we want a change in the way our team, organisation or family treats time, then we need patience, persistence and determination. If we have those qualities then we might as well be the one to start the revolution.

8 ways to be small but smart

Find a buddy

If you are in a group or an organisation where you feel things aren't right then you are unlikely to be alone. Seek out like-minded people. Your colleagues will fall into three categories: those who agree but aren't willing to do anything about it; those who agree and would be willing to act; and those who don't think there is a problem. It is the second group, however small, who are going to make your campaign a success - so focus on them.

Be consistent

In a psychological experiment, participants were asked to look at a series of slides that were all different shades of blue, and say whether they were blue or green. In the group were two stooges who were on the side of the experimenter. When they were consistent in their agreement with each other, the rest of the group was more inclined to vary their view and agree with them, even when they gave a blatantly incorrect answer. Consistency creates converts.

Show your conviction (don't just talk about it)

When those trying to create change are seen to put in personal time and effort, they are far more successful at persuading others to join in their crusade. Passion is infectious.

Be one of the group but not one of the crowd

If we are seen to be out of the group then our views and actions won't have much impact. Given that we are behaving differently about how we treat time, we need to make it clear elsewhere that we are still part of the group.

Token gestures count

During the 1960s in the United States, those fighting for equal rights for the black population used a technique known as 'frown power'. When someone did or said something that went against your values, you frowned - an overt show of disapproval without conflict. Whilst this alone will not be enough to change a culture, it is many small steps like these that start to get the change rolling.

Encouragement

Pick up one new supporter at a time. Give praise for punctual time keeping, quick decisions and considered requests and explain the positive impact the actions had. Let the consensus emerge of its own accord.

Don't blame the boss

One individual doesn't control a culture. The people at the top can influence but the community decides. Don't expect all the change to come from above.

Pay attention

With every new decision, experience and additional person joining, cultures change. Perhaps imperceptibly, but they change nonetheless. As a result, they need continuous nurturing. Keep aware of what is going on.

Changing the time culture

1 I spend all my time in meetings

It doesn't have to be a business: get togethers, check-ins, talks about talks and steering groups can take hold everywhere from the local authority council chamber to the cycling club, the babysitting circle, the theatre group, the wine tasters and the ramblers. Even book clubs have been known to collapse under the weight of discussion about which book they should read.

At the heart of a meetings culture there's usually a lack of clarity about how decisions should be made. Who needs to be asked for their views? Does everyone need to agree? Who gets to have the final say so? If we don't know we are likely to get bogged down in endless cross checking and base covering. All of which requires a lot of meetings and a lot of time.

> ## Anyone else got anything they'd like to add?
>
> The most successful clothes shops spot an emerging trend, they design and manufacture the right garments, and then get them onto coat hangers in a few weeks. One fashion retailer The Mind Gym worked with was battling to get their products to market in eight months. The reason why? Each new design had to pass through a long line of approvals. By the time everyone had had their say, either the trend had passed or the competition had got there ahead of them, or both. A clear case of the ends getting lost in the means.

The remedies

- **Decide who decides**

    Start new projects by developing a grid that lists the main decisions that will need to be made. The team involved can then decide together who is responsible for which decision and whom they should consult.

    A magazine editor and her team used this system to analyse their production process. They found that even the smallest decisions were being referred back to the editor. As a result the magazine's time to press was taking much longer than it should have been, leaving the final hours before publication a roller coaster ride of panic. The team simplified the process by clarifying which decisions should be taken where, delegating decisions about, for example, picture content to the picture editor and leaving the editor with responsibility for the overall style.

- **Delegate decisions**

    When we ask someone to do something, we should also be clear what decisions they are free to make on their own and what we want to be asked about first. Similarly, when we're taking on a task for someone else we should clarify what decisions we can make on our own.

- **Narrow questions**

    Consultation can start with, 'What do you think about the web problem?' or alternatively, 'We've currently got one area of the site no one seems to find. Do you think we should promote it more heavily, change the theme or lose it altogether?' The more precise the question, the quicker the meeting is likely to be.

- **Consultation without meetings**

    Faster and much less hassle than a meeting is electronic consultation. There are numerous options from invitation-only forums to voting buttons on email. If you have specific questions on an issue you could introduce a system of 'consultation windows', where people who might have a contribution to make are asked to comment by a specific time. Again, this works best when the questions are fairly specific.

2 'Another working party'

Peter, a long standing Board member of a global organisation recalled being asked to join the Mission Committee. When he asked what this committee was for, he was told, 'to decide on the purpose of the organisation'. He declined, feeling that if they didn't know after the 30 successful years he'd been involved with the organisation, a mission committee wasn't going to come up with the answer.

Along with a love of meetings, comes a love of a particular type of meeting. In some cultures the answer to any problem is to create a forum, committee, working party, project team or some other extra bit of 'process'.

As with many of the time culture problems, the intention is a good one: to get a group of experts together to solve a problem. However, when it is over-done the consequence is an abundance of activity with relatively little to show for it.

Remedies

- **Tighten the deadlines**

  When less time is available people are forced into rapid decision making rather than rambling process.

- **Solve it now**

  Process can be a cop out. Don't give in to mental lethargy - see if the problem can be solved right here, right now, whether you're on the train, plane or walking to a meeting.

- **Get the right people in the room to begin with**

  Process is often long winded because we start something without thinking through who needs to be involved. Make an effort to get the right people into the discussion from the off and you should be able to wind things up quickly.

- **Agree the whole process up front**

  Design and agree the whole journey, from soup to nuts, before it starts. This way there should be fewer talks about talks and more getting on with addressing the primary concern.

- **Limit number of meetings per month**

  One FTSE-100 business has limited the number of meetings someone can go to in a week. Some companies have very few meeting rooms - others don't have chairs. The idea is that if the facilities aren't available people will have to get the talking and the decision making out of the way in one go, rather than endlessly reconvening.

3 'I can never get on with my own work'

Even more than the other time destroying cultures, this one starts off with the very best of intentions: help thy neighbour. If I'm stuck, I ask you and you help me out. The favour is returned. Communication is open, the spirit is co-operative and we are likely to be unproductive, at least initially.

But too much of anything can be a bad thing and this particular time culture has got out of hand when being a good team player top trumps getting your head down and battling on: when we can't complete anything because we have to deal with constant unpredictable requests for our time, it's time to act.

This way of working can also lead to another time destroying culture, long hours, when we find ourselves working more and more extreme hours to get the peace and quiet we need to complete our own projects.

And it's not just a problem of office life - anyone who works with the public or with children will know what it feels like to have no time to yourself.

The challenge, of course, is how to wrestle back some control, whilst retaining all the good parts of a communicative and co-operative culture.

Remedy

Sometimes we have to take drastic actions. Here is how some other people have found time to call their own:

- **Introduce quiet time**

  When a British supermarket introduced open plan offices they discovered many benefits but one loud complaint: constant interruptions. The solution was to give everyone a red hat that they wore to signal that they weren't to be interrupted.

  A software design company that had a problem with interruptions introduced a 'Quiet Time' policy. This was an hour a day, in everyone's diaries, when interruptions were banned. Scheduling the Quiet Time was key. Just as important as getting more time to themselves was the fact that people were no longer expecting interruptions and so they could relax and concentrate properly. The consequence was both a great increase in productivity and a marked decline in hours worked, which made everyone happy.

  A friend of The Mind Gym described the home equivalent of quiet time. He and his wife had five young children, usually playing, occasionally fighting and always demanding their parents' attention. The couple, at their wits' end, created a 'cocktail hour'. The deal was that during this hour there were to be no interruptions, questions or requests - this was time set aside for Mum and Dad to spend alone together. The children were allowed to interrupt in a serious emergency, like a broken limb, but otherwise the house was quiet. It worked and the couple attributed much of the success of their relationship to the introduction of the cocktail hour.

4 Long hours and getting longer

Long hours can be a good thing if it means we get lots done quickly and then, maybe, take a well-earned break. The danger occurs when, as in the example we saw earlier, people stay around just to be seen.

Parkinson's law states that work expands to fill the time available. This means that if we have three hours to change a light bulb, it will more than likely take three hours - on our way to the light socket we might take the opportunity to sort out the cupboard under the stairs, then fix the wonky step on the ladder, clean the lampshade, check the fuse and maybe decide to give the ceiling a fresh coat of paint whilst we're up there. Well, if we're not in a hurry, why not? The trouble is, whilst we may not be in a hurry, there may well be better things that we could be doing rather than hanging around putting in 'face time'.

Remedies

- **Talk about results not effort**

  Encourage people to separate quality from quantity. It's a common time trap to see the length of time something takes as an indication of its value. But that's a dangerous, time consuming illusion. Get round it by asking people to describe the outcome they want and resist asking 'how long should this take?'

- **Start a movement**

  One food business turns off the lights in their offices at 6 o'clock each evening to ensure that people go home. This may remove choice but it certainly discourages a late hours culture. If we want to keep our friends then turning off the lights (or the coffee machine) may not be so popular but we could get together with colleagues and decide our own policy: united we leave on time.

- **Recognise people who are doing it**

  If you are in a position where you can praise people for their behaviour, then recognise those who leave promptly. Make heroes and heroines of those who achieve great things in normal hours rather than those who have slaved through the night (and take two days off to recover).

Ready for the revolution?

Toxic time cultures are just bad habits that a lot of people have signed up to. As with nail biting and eating junk food they are habits that can be given up. Like the monkeys avoiding the cold shower, they might have started out as useful behaviours but, if they have become outdated and counterproductive, they need to be changed.

It takes a little imagination to realise that things can be done differently and may take some considerable determination to see the changes through but, if you want more and better time, the rewards will be worth it.

So go on, make the first move.

Go get that banana.

The beginning of time

Is this book good value for money?

Perhaps you haven't decided yet. When you do, it will depend on what you were hoping for in the first place. Perhaps you wanted to tackle a specific problem, or were looking to pick up some useful tips, or fancied something easy to read on the train, or you simply thought the colour of the cover would cheer up a dull day. Whatever your reason, if this book provides you with what you want you will probably decide that it is good value. And if it hasn't done so yet, well, let's hope this final section does the trick.

We are constantly making judgements about whether something is good or bad value for money. Sometimes the judgement is automatic and we aren't even aware that we're doing it - like choosing where to buy our morning coffee. At other times it takes just a few seconds - upper circle or stalls?

If we need to cut back our spending or if we suddenly get a windfall, it's relatively easy to re-calibrate what we think is good or poor value for funds. Then we can head off spending or scrimping accordingly.

But when it comes to judging value for time we are rarely so aware, or so skilled. As a result, we sometimes make bad decisions about how to spend our time, if we make any conscious decision at all.

The techniques in this book are designed to make us more aware, or mindful, about how we spend our time. In isolation they work well and combined together they can have a magnificent effect. But to get the benefit we need to spot when our time is being poorly used in the first place. And not just once but always.

The answer is to use a kind of 'time antennae' which keep us alert to how well our time is being used. The rest of this chapter is about how to develop these time antennae.

Potentially, it offers a new beginning of time, or, at least, how we use it.

A penny for your quartz

The first step to developing time sense is to establish a currency of time. This currency consists of two simple elements:

Time generators: These are things or people which enable us to achieve as much - or more - than we consider reasonable for the amount of time that has been used.

Time parasites: These are things or people that give us a worse return on our time than we think reasonable.

Of course, in the same way that value for money is usually a matter of opinion, so is value for time. So whether you consider something a time parasite or a time generator is entirely up to you. Is half an hour surfing the internet research (a generator), a way of avoiding dull but necessary paperwork (a parasite), or relaxation (could be either). Only you know the answer.

Parasitium Maternum

Q: Is my mother a parasite?

A: Possibly, it depends on circum-stances.

If your mother keeps calling and inter-rupting your work or taking your attention off a complicated task, she could be a parasite. If, however, regular contact with your family is something you cherish then your mother's phone calls are helping you achieve something important. Similarly, if she rings at the end of a long day and you have a good laugh together, her calls could help you relax and reduce your stress levels - definitely a valuable time generator.

Q: Can a parasite ever become a generator?

A: Absolutely.

Picture Tim as he arrives at the station to catch his regular evening train. He stands on the platform with a crowd of other agitated commuters, all staring fixedly at the departures board. After a few moments the screen clears and a message scrolls across announcing a delay of at least forty-five minutes to the next train. A groan goes up. Disgruntled passengers check their watches and start making calls. Nobody punches the air yelling 'Great, a whole forty-five minutes to spend in the fast food court' because, from the look of it, nobody's feeling that way. The late train is a time parasite, no question about it.

Tim mooches around killing time and whilst he's browsing the magazine stand he bumps into the sister of an old school friend. They go for a drink, get on famously and fix up a date for the following weekend. Suddenly a frustrating delay and time parasite has turned into a lucky encounter and time generator.

Does this way of thinking actually help?

Many workout participants seem to think so.

- When you visit an art gallery, how much time do you spend reading the information panels versus looking at the pictures? One workout participant realised that she spent at least as much time on the words as taking in what they were describing. For her, what was supposed to be a time generator - to help her get more out of the paintings - had become a time parasite: it was preventing her from looking at the paintings themselves. She now ignores all the panels and feels that, as a result, her time at exhibitions is much better spent.

- When you are lost, do you stop the car to ask for directions? Or do you carry on driving, trusting your innate sense of direction and good fortune to get you back on the right route? One participant used the idea of parasites and generators to convince his partner that stopping for two minutes was more likely to be a time generator than carrying on for another two minutes. They carried out an experiment; both asking for advice and carrying on driving on five separate occasions. When they measured the impact they concluded that asking for advice generally paid a generous time dividend.

- A restaurant guide should be a time generator. One participant realised they weren't helping him when, after several disappointing meals, he booked a table at a restaurant that was described as romantic and full of charm only to find it kitsch and full of tourists. Now he asks friends who share his tastes in restaurants for their recommendations, which, though it takes longer, he feels gives a much better return.

- A regular meeting for a new team can be a great time generator, allowing communication to flow quickly and accurately. A participant recalled setting up a Monday gathering for her team. It was very popular and everyone agreed that it saved time in the rest of the week. A year later things had moved on but the meeting had remained the same and now the participants were just going through the motions. The meeting had become a parasite rather than a generator. Having spotted what was happening, she revamped the meeting to focus on more relevant issues.

Getting engaged

If you made it to the final chapter of 'The Mind Gym: wake your mind up' you will recognise this chart:

	Internal	External
Helpful	Thinking	Engaged
Harmful	Critical	Autopilot

Its purpose is to show four different states that our mind moves between. For those who aren't familiar with it, here is a brief explanation.

In the left hand column our focus is internal. On these occasions it can feel like we are talking to ourselves or, at the very least, we are aware of what we are thinking. If you just thought 'what on earth do they mean by that?' - there's an example.

Sometimes these conversations aren't very helpful. We berate our-selves with harsh judgements: 'that was a stupid thing of me to do' or 'why did I just waste my time on something so silly?' This kind of self talk is called 'Critical'. At other times the conversation in our head is helpful: 'I can use the lessons from last time' or 'what would happen if I tried it this way?' This state is called, somewhat literally, 'Constructive thinking' or, for short, 'thinking'.

For psychology buffs, 'Critical' is similar to Timothy Gallwey's 'self 1' and 'Thinking' is similar to Ellen Langer's 'mindfulness'.

In the right column our focus is external. On these occasions we aren't aware of what we're thinking - we're just doing it. If, for exam-ple, we crack a joke straight out, then our focus is external. We may even surprise ourself with our spontaneous wit. If, however, we ask 'will they think this is funny?' or run the joke through in our head before saying it, then our focus is internal.

Again, the external focus can be helpful or harmful.

Sometimes we slip into autopilot. We are simply going through the motions, oblivious to what we are doing. For every day tasks, like brushing our teeth or filling the kettle, this may not be important. But the danger is that we end up doing the wrong things, or the right things in the wrong way, and yet carry on none the wiser. The participant who continues reading the information panels in the art gallery even though it was detracting from her visits, was in auto-pilot. Until she realised the impact: at that moment she moved into 'thinking'.

When we are on top form we are usually fully immersed in what we are doing. If you ski or play golf, or any other physical activity that demands concentration, you will probably remember moments when you felt totally absorbed in what you were doing. This is what is meant by being 'engaged'. When this happens your sense of time may seem distorted: you make it to the bottom of the slope in what feels like only a few seconds, or the moment you kick the ball into the top left corner of the net seems to last forever.

To put this in the language of academic psychology, 'Engaged' is similar to Csikszentmihalyi's 'flow' and Gallwey's 'self 2', and 'Autopilot' is akin to Langer's 'mindlessness'.

To the music of time

Ideally, we want to remain entirely in the top row, moving between 'thinking' and 'engaged'. At one moment we consider our options and decide which one to follow, and then we get on and do it, completely immersed in our chosen route. We shift back to 'thinking' occasionally to check everything is going fine, or to work out an alternative if it isn't, and then we're back in the thick of it, externally focused and completely engaged.

At its best, it feels like we are dancing between these two states.

The concept of parasites and generators is designed to help move us into 'thinking' mode. By asking ourselves, 'at this moment, is what I am doing a parasite or a generator?' we force our minds to focus internally. We can then make a considered judgement and, if we find that we are involved with a parasite, we can choose how to deal with it. We might decide to say 'no' to something, put the magazine aside and get back to the job in hand, or find a way to steer our conversation on to something more productive than last night's movie.

We may not stay in 'thinking' mode for long. Just long enough to make a wise call on how our time is being spent and decide what, if anything, to do about it.

Out of autopilot

When it comes to wasting time, autopilot is the most dangerous place to be.

Routines lure us into autopilot. It's very easy to adopt a routine for a perfectly good reason and then stick with it, long after the original reason has ceased to apply. Like the woman with the redundant Monday morning meeting we carry on doing the same thing that we have always done without ever assessing whether this is still a good use of our time.

When our time antennae are switched on, we become alert to potential parasites like these and are more likely to snap out of autopilot and into 'thinking'. And once we're thinking, we can move on to more productive activities.

Up and running

To get your time antennae working, start by checking in with yourself regularly. Set a reminder for every hour of the day; the alarm on your computer, perhaps, or the countdown timer on your mobile. Every time it goes off, check with yourself and ask: 'Is what I'm doing a Time Generator or a Time Parasite?'

If that question isn't precise enough, then try: 'Bearing in mind what I want to achieve, is what I am currently doing providing a better or worse return on my time than I consider reasonable?' Remember, you decide what is 'reasonable'.

At first it may be difficult to judge, but don't let that worry you. What matters is that you get used to asking the question - the more often the better. Simply by pausing long enough to consider whether our time is being well spent, we gain control.

Sometimes the answer will be obvious. At other times, things may not be so clear cut and we may want to suspend judgement and reconsider later. And remember, just because something has been a time parasite in the past doesn't mean it will be this time.

A member of The Mind Gym tried this out. She found a watch that vibrated at regular intervals, originally designed for people without sight, and wore it for a day. When it went off, which it did every 30 minutes, she asked herself 'was the last half an hour a time parasite or a time generator?'

'It was odd', she explained, 'I thought about time more during that day than I normally do in a month. It was quite disruptive to start with and I certainly wouldn't want to do it every day. But it did make me much more conscious of time. It had several long term benefits. It made me aware of time parasites early on, so I could act on them before they ate up too much time. And, because I was analysing my time so thoroughly, I became much more disciplined about using it well. Even though I have never worn the watch again, I think much more often about how well I am using my time and, as a result, make better decisions about what to do with it.'

10 time parasites

1. A sick computer
2. An empty fridge
3. A long queue
4. Bad filing
5. Lost keys
6. A mislaid remote control unit
7. An empty rechargeable battery
8. A niggling worry
9. A request for help
10. Listening (poorly)

10 time generators

1. The off switch on your phone
2. The shortcut menu on your PC
3. A course in touch typing
4. The traffic update service on your car radio
5. A notebook
6. The spell check button
7. www.tpsonline.org.uk (service that enables you to block cold calls)
8. www.mpsonline.org.uk (same thing for junk mail)
9. A request for help (yes, it can be either)
10. Listening (well)

Accurate reading

The more we pay attention to how our time is being used, the more savvy our antennae become. We build up a data bank of past parasites and generators and so our assessments become faster and more accurate. Was searching for medical advice on the web a help or a waste? Was that hour on the phone to the nurse a parasite or a generator? Was the homeopathic course worth the effort?

To build up this personal data bank of generators and parasites we need to reflect on past experiences as well as check in on the current ones.

At the end of each day ask: what were my great time generators today? And the biggest time parasites? Even better, write down the answers (or record them online) and see what patterns emerge.

One workout participant discovered that checking email was his biggest parasite. He now checks it only every two hours. Another participant reflected on making her colleagues tea or coffee. Once in a while this was a kind thing to do and reinforced her desire to be helpful and supportive; but she was doing it so often that the benefit was diluted and she had less and less time to get on with her own work.

When we reflect on what has and has not proved to be a good use of our time, we increase our chances of making wise decisions in future. But don't pore over it for hours otherwise you will be creating another time parasite. Reflection of this kind is best when it is quick but frequent.

Time up

When people complained that life was too short, the Roman philosopher Seneca replied that their problem wasn't with the amount of time but with how they used it.

Two thousand years later our life expectancy may have trebled but the complaints about lack of time are much the same. And so, in many respects, is the answer.

The big advantage we have over the senator with his sundial, is that we now know a lot more. There is extensive, rigorous research that yields profound insights about how the human mind works, there are diagnostic tools that unveil the mysteries of how we think, and we have a wealth of time enhancing tools that have been tested, revised and tested again. Of course, we may not use them. But if we do, we are equipped to make much more informed decisions about how to make the best use of time than any previous generation.

This book is very far from being the sum of wisdom on the subject. There is, for a start, a wealth of provocative and enlightening books and papers, many of which are listed in the references on the following pages.

Those who prefer a more dynamic route can explore a variety of tools and questionnaires, as well as the minds of tens of thousands of interested, and usually interesting, members at The Mind Gym Online (you can also send your questionnaires to friends to see how their views compare with yours). If you haven't discovered it already, your membership code is in the inside cover.

All of this should help. But don't expect revolution: instead prepare for evolution.

We can change our habits about time, over time. But very rarely can we change them overnight. A makeover of any kind consists of lots of little changes. Some of these give immediate gains, others take longer to show any benefit and a few may not work at all.

A member of The Mind Gym likened this to the following story from a speech at a wedding, given by the father of the bride.

'Almost thirty-five years ago today, Angela and I were married. On the day before the ceremony we made our own secret pact and it was this: that throughout our married life, whatever would happen, I would make all the big decisions and Angela would make all the little ones.

'I am pleased to report that thirty-five years on we are still blissfully married and that throughout that time we have stuck firmly to our agreement. I can also reveal that during these last thirty-five years', he paused, 'there have been no big decisions.'

And so it is with transforming our lives so we feel fantastic about time and how we spend it: no big decisions and lots of little ones. You may see this as a great adventure filled with rich discoveries and powerful insights, or as a test of endurance against the powers of apathy and resignation. However you take on the challenge, it is yours to navigate, to experiment with and to enjoy.

Take your time.

References

Abernathy, D. J. (1999). *'A get-real guide to time management.'* Training & Development 53(6): 22-+.

Accountemps (2002). Press release: Thank goodness it's Tuesday.

Archer, N., D. Robilliard, et al. (2003). *'A length polymorphism in the circadian clock gene per3 is linked to delayed sleep phase syndrome and extreme diurnal preference.'* SLEEP 26: 413 - 415.

Atkinson, G. and T. Relly (1996). *'Circadian variation in sports performance.'* Sports Med 21(4): 292 - 312.

Avni-Babad, D. and I. Ritov (2003). *'Routine and the perception of time.'* Journal Of Experimental Psychology - General 132(4): 543 - 550.

Baltes, B. B. and H. A. Heydens-Gahir (2003). *'Reduction of work-family conflict through the use of selection, optimization, and compensation behaviors.'* Journal Of Applied Psychology 88(6): 1005 - 1018.

Barling, J., E. K. Kelloway, et al. (1996). *'Time management and achievement striving interact to predict car sales performance.'* Journal Of Applied Psychology 81(6): 821 - 826.

Bee, F., R. Bee, et al. (1998). *Facilitation skills.* London, Institute of Personnel and Development.

Berglas, S. (2004). 'Chronic time abuse.' Harvard Business Review 82(6): 90

Bluedorn, A. C. (2002). *The human organization of time: temporal realities and experience.* Stanford, Calif., Stanford Business Books.

Bluedorn, A. C. and E. T. Hall (1998). *'An interview with anthropologist Edward T. Hall.'* Journal Of Management Inquiry 7(2): 109 - 115.

Bluedorn, A. C., D. B. Turban, et al. (1999). 'The effects of stand-up and sit-down meeting formats on meeting outcomes.' Journal Of Applied Psychology 84(2): 277 - 285.

Brozo, W. G. and J. L. Johns (1986). 'A content and critical analysis of 40 speed reading books.' Journal of Reading 30(3): 242 - 247.

Buehler, R. and D. Griffin (2003). 'Planning, personality, and prediction: The role of future focus in optimistic time predictions.' Organizational Behavior And Human Decision Processes 92(1 - 2): 80 - 90.

Buehler, R., D. Griffin, et al. (1994). 'Exploring The Planning Fallacy - Why People Underestimate Their Task Completion Times.' Journal Of Personality And Social Psychology 67(3): 366 - 381.

Bull, P. E. (1994). 'On identifying questions, replies and nonreplies in political interviews.' Journal of Language and Social Psychology 13: 115 - 131.

Bull, P. E. (2003). The microanalysis of political communication: Claptrap and ambiguity. London: Routledge.

Bull, P. E. and K. Mayer (1993). 'How not to answer questions in political interviews.' Political Psychology 14: 651 - 666.

Burka Jane, B. and Lenora M. Yuen (1983). Procrastination: why you do it, what to do about it. Reading, MA, Addison Wesley Pub. Co.

Burt, C. D. B. and S. Kemp (1994). 'Construction Of Activity Duration And Time Management Potential.' Applied Cognitive Psychology 8(2): 155 - 168.

Buysse, D., B. Barzansky, et al. (2002). 'Sleep, Fatigue, and Medical Training: Setting an Agenda for Optimal Learning and Patient Care.' SLEEP 26: 218 - 225.

Cialdini, R. B. (2001). Influence: science and practice. Boston, Mass.; London, Allyn and Bacon.

Claxton, G. (1998). Hare brain, tortoise mind: why intelligence increases when you think less. London, Fourth Estate.

Claxton, G. (2000). Wise up: the challenge of lifelong learning. London, Bloomsbury.

Conte, J. M., J. E. Mathieu, et al. (1998). 'The nomological and predictive validity of time urgency.' Journal Of Organizational Behavior 19(1): 1 - 13.

Csikszentmihalyi, M. (1991). Flow: the psychology of optimal experience. New York, Harper Perennial.

Csikszentmihalyi, M. and I. S. Csikszentmihalyi (1992). Optimal experience: psychological studies of flow in consciousness. Cambridge, University Press.

Deci, E. L. (1975). Intrinsic motivation. New York; London, Plenum Press.

Dilts, R. B. (1994). *Strategies of genius.* Capitola, Calif., Meta Publications.

Dryden, W. (2000). *Overcoming procrastination.* London, Sheldon.

Ellis, A. and W. Dryden (1999). *The practice of REBT.* London, Free Assocation.

Erbaugh, S. J. and M. L. Barnett (1986). *'Effects of modelling and goal-setting on the jumping performance of primary-grade children.'* Perceptual and Motor Skills 63:1287 - 1293.

Erez, M. and I. Zidon (1984). *'Effects of goal acceptance on the relationship of goal setting and task performance.'* Journal of Applied Psychology 69: 69 - 78.

Fensterheim, H. and J. Baer (1993). *Don't say yes when you want to say no.* London, Warner.

Fontana, D. (1993). *Managing time.* Leicester, British Psychological Society.

Foster, R. G. and L. Kreitzman (2004). *Rhythms of life: the biological clocks that control the daily lives of every living thing.* London, Profile Books.

Furnham, A. (1996). *Lay theories: everyday understanding of problems in the social sciences.* London, Whurr Publishers, 1996.

Furnham, A. (2005). *The psychology of behaviour at work: the individual in the organisation.* New York, NY, Psychology Press.

Gale, C. and C. Martyn (1998). *'Larks and owls and health, wealth, and wisdom.'* British Medical Journal 317(7174): 1675 - 1677.

Gladwell, M. (2005). *Blink.* Allen Lane.

Karsten, A. (1928). *'Mental Satiation' in Field Theory as Human Science.* Ed. J. de Rivera (New York: Gardner Press, 1976).

Kaufman-Scarborough, C. and J. D. Lindquist (1999). *'Time Management and Polychronicity: Comparisons, Contrasts, and Insights for the Workplace.'* Journal of Managerial Psychology 14(3): 288 - 312.

Kay, J. (1998). *Why the last shall be first and the first shall fade away.* Financial Times, London.

Kelly, W. E. (2003). *'No time to worry: the relationship between worry, time structure, and time management.'* Personality And Individual Differences 35(5): 1119 - 1126.

Kripke, D. F., L. Garfinkel, et al. (2002). *'Mortality associated with sleep duration and insomnia.'* Archives Of General Psychiatry 59(2): 131 - 136.

Landy, F. J., H. Rastegary, et al. (1991). *'Time Urgency - The Construct And Its Measurement.'* Journal Of Applied Psychology 76(5): 644 - 657.

Langer, E. J. (1991). *Mindfulness: choice and control in everyday life.* London, Collins-Harvill.

Langer, E. J. (1997) *The Power of Mindful Learning.* A Merloyd Lawrence Book.

Latham, G. P. and J. J. Baldes (1975). *'The 'Practical Significance' of Locke's Theory of Goal Setting.'* Journal of Applied Psychology. 60(3): 122 - 124.

Lay, C. H. and H. C. Schouwenburg (1993). *'Trait Procrastination, Time Management, And Academic Behavior.'* Journal Of Social Behavior And Personality 8(4): 647 - 662.

Layard, R. (2005). *Happiness: Lessons from a new science.* Allen Lane.

Lefton, L. A., R. J. Nagle, G. Johnson and D. F. Fisher (1979). *'Eye movement dynamics of good and poor readers: then and now.'* Journal of Reading Behavior 11: 319 - 328.

Levinson, W., D. L. Roter, et al. (1997). *'Physician-patient communication - The relationship with malpractice claims among primary care physicians and surgeons.'* Jama-Journal Of The American Medical Association 277(7): 553 - 559.

Levitt, S. D. and S. J. Dubner (2005). *Freakonomics: a rogue economist explores the hidden side of everything.* London, Allen Lane.

Locke, E. A. (1968). *'Theory of task motivation and incentives.'* Organizational behavior and human performance 3(2): 157.

Locke, E. A. (2004). *The Blackwell handbook of principles of organizational behavior.* Oxford, Blackwell.

Locke, E. A. and G. P. Latham (2002). *'Building a practically useful theory of goal setting and task motivation - A 35-year odyssey.'* American Psychologist 57(9): 705 - 717.

Luong, A. & S. G. Rogelberg (2005). *'Meetings and More Meetings: The Relationship Between Meeting Load and the Daily Well-being of Employees.'* Group Dynamics: Theory, Research, and Practice. 9(1): 58 - 67.

Macan, T. H. (1994). *'Time Management - Test Of A Process Model.'* Journal Of Applied Psychology 79(3): 381 - 391.

Macan, T. H. (1996). *'Time-management training: Effects on time behaviors, attitudes, and job performance.'* Journal Of Psychology 130(3): 229 - 236.

Macan, T. H., C. Shahani, et al. (1990). *'College-Students' Time Management - Correlations With Academic Performance And Stress.'* Journal Of Educational Psychology 82(4): 760 - 768.

McCormack, M. H. (1986). *What they don't teach you at Harvard Business School.* Glasgow, Fontana.

McGrath, J. E. and J. R. Kelly (1986). *Time and human interaction: toward a social psychology of time.* New York; London, Guilford Press.

Miller, C. C. and L. B. Cardinal (1994). *'Strategic-Planning And Firm Performance - A Synthesis Of More Than 2 Decades Of Research.'* Academy Of Management Journal 37(6): 1649 - 1665.

Persing, D. L. (1993). *The Influence of Temporal Allocation Information on Perceptions of Software Engineers and Evaluations of Their Work.*

Razran, G. H. S. (1940). *'Conditioning away social bias by the luncheon technique.'* Psychological Bulletin 35: 481.

Robinson, S. L. and D. M. Rousseau (1994). *'Violating The Psychological Contract - Not The Exception But The Norm.'* Journal Of Organizational Behavior 15(3): 245 - 259.

Rosenman, R. H. and M. Friedman (1974). *'Neurogenic Factors In Pathogenesis Of Coronary Heart-Disease.'* Medical Clinics Of North America 58(2): 269 - 279.

Seiwert, L. (1991). *Time is money.* London, Kogan Page.

Seligman, M. E. P. (2003). *Authentic happiness: using the new positive psychology to realise your potential for lasting fulfilment.* London, Nicholas Brealey.

Smith, H. (1994). *The 10 natural laws of successful time and life management.* New York, Warner Books.

Smolensky, M. H. (1998). *'Knowledge and attitudes of American physicians and public about medical chronobiology and chronotherapeutics. Findings of two 1996 Gallup surveys.'* Chronobiology International 15(4): 377 - 394.

Smolensky, M. H. and L. Lamberg (2001). *The body clock guide to better health: how to use your body's natural clock to fight illness and achieve maximum health.* New York, Henry Holt.

Smulders, S. (1990). *'Control of freeway traffic flow by variable speed signs.'* Transportation Research 24(2): 111.

Thomas E. L. and H. A. Robinson (1982). *Improving reading in every class.* Boston, Allyn & Bacon.

Thomas, K. E., S. E. Newstead, et al. (2003). *'Exploring the time prediction process: The effects of task experience and complexity on prediction accuracy.'* Applied Cognitive Psychology 17(6): 655 - 673.

Westcott, W. (1994). *'Exercise speed and strength development.'* American Fitness Quarterly 13(3): 20 - 21.

Wrzesniewski, A., McCauley, C. R., Rozin, P., and Schwartz, B. (1997). *'Jobs, careers and callings: People's relations to their work.'* Journal of Research in Personality 31: 21 - 33.

Zakor, H. (1979). *'Concept of influencing speed on motorways by a control system which depends on the situation.'* Strassen und Autobahn 30(6): 243.

Index

action plans, 32
advertisers, 93
afternoon person see Owls
agile techniques, 160–2
airport check-in, 152, 154–5
alarm call and rushaholics, 63–4
anchoring, 63
Antrim, Minna, 49
anxious person, 165, 167–8
assistance, belief in, 81
asthma sufferers, 68
autopilot, 254, 255
    switching off when dealing with
        interruptions, 160–2

beliefs, unconscious, 77–86, 145
    leading to procrastination, 80–3
    quick fixes to changing, 84–6
    rethinking unhelpful, 83–4
Berne, Eric, 4, 146
biological day and night, 69
Bluedorn, Allen, 39, 213
boredom, 163
bosses, what they want from
    employees, 235
burnout, 148–9
busy, being 25–7, 145–6 see also Doves;
    Hawks
Buysse, Daniel, 74

capability delegation, 224–5, 226, 227,
    229
Cartland, Dame Barbara, 67
certainty, belief in, 80–1
challenge
    balancing with skill in goal getting,
        116–17

combining with meaning, 96
combining with pleasure, 95
as source of happiness, 90–1, 95–6,
    99, 100, 101–2
chapter summaries, 18–19
chatty person, 166, 168–9
checklists, 41
Claxton, Guy, 148
Cognitive Behavioural Therapy, 78
Coleridge, Samuel Taylor, 156
committees, 245–6
concentration curve, 67–76
    and genes, 71
    and Hummingbirds, 71–2
    and Larks, 69–70, 73
    and Owls, 70, 73
    plotting your own, 75
    reshaping our daily routine to fit,
        72–5
contracts, psychological, 229
control, 2
    exercise to achieve, 49–52
    external and internal locus of, 50, 51
controlling person, 166, 171
critical self-talk, 254
Csikszentmihalyi, Mihaly, 91, 96, 115,
    254
cultures, 240 see also time cultures

day, biological, 69
dead time, 150–5
deadlines, 2, 40, 246
decision-making, 233
    and rushaholics, 61
    split-second, 53
    and spontaneous people/planners,
        35

delegation, 148, 170, 221–9, 245
    capability, 224–5, 226, 227, 229
    fears and suggestions, 228
    optimum strategy, 226–7
    precision, 222–4, 226, 227, 229
demand, being in, 147
dental surgeries, 39
diaries, 32, 145
Dilts, Robert, 133
direction-setting exercise, 104–12
Disney, Walt, 133
doctors suing of by patients, 56–7
Doves, 26–7, 27–8
    resigned and striving, 28, 29
    turning Hawks into, 29–31
drifting, 162–3
driving fast, 55–6
duties, 97

ease, belief in, 82–3
eating and rushing, 62–3
efficiency and saying no, 174
ego, appealing to, 232–3
electronic consultation, 245
Ellis, Albert, 78, 83
empathy, 166, 175
'engaged', 254, 255
estimating how long something will
    take, 64
external focus, 254
external locus of control, 50
eye jumps whilst reading, 187–8

'face time', 241, 248
failure, immunity from, 81
family and direction-setting exercise,
    108
finance and direction-setting exercise,
    107
fitness training, 56
fixations and speed reading, 193–4, 199
flow, 26, 113–14, 116–18, 119, 120–2,
    254
food
    association with likeability, 234
    rushing when eating, 63–4
free me up programme, 9, 11
freedom, belief in, 82
Friedman, Meyer, 60
'frown power', 243
Furnham, Adrian, 233

Gallwey, Timothy, 254
game, treating life as a, 30
generators see time generators
getting up late in morning, 64–5
getting on with your own work, 246–8

Gladwell, Malcolm Blink, 53
goal getting, 113–22
    advantages, 114–15
    balancing skill with challenge, 116–18
    need for stretching without strain,
        117–18
    setting a flow friendly goal, 118–19
    staying in flow, 120–2
    ways to increase motivation in,
        119–20
goals ways of reducing, 142–5
'good time manager', 54
good works, 96
grinding to a halt, 151–2, 154
Grisham, John, 49

Hall, Edmund, 39
hanging on, 151, 154
happiness, 2, 89–102
    challenge as source, 90–1, 95–6, 99,
        100, 101–2
    combining sources, 92–9
    meaning as source, 91–2, 97–8, 99,
        100, 102
    pleasure as source of, 90, 93–5, 99,
        100, 101
    ways of increasing, 99–102
    and wealth, 89
happy days programme, 9, 12
'Harried' game, 146–7
Hawks, 27
    striving and resigned, 28
    turning into Doves, 29–31
heart attacks, 60
hedonism, 92–4
hedonistic treadmill, 93
Henman, Tim, 157
hold-ups, 151–2, 154
Hummingbirds, 71–2
hurrying up see rushaholics

immersion, 2
immersion planning see visualisation
immunity from failure, belief in, 81
indecisive person, 165, 166–7
internal focus, 253–4, 255
internal locus of control, 50
interruptions, 4, 35, 156–64, 247
Ivanisevic, Goran, 157

Johnson, Samuel, 124
journal, keeping a, 49
judge, rushing to, 61–2

Karsten, Anita, 164
Kay, Professor John, 66
Kelly, Janice, 121

Kinnock, Neil, 179–80

labels, time, 46–54
   'good time manager', 54
   'my time isn't my own', 49–52
   relativity, 52
   time = quality, 53–4
   work, 47–9
Langer, Ellen, 47, 254
Larkin, Philip, 155
Larks, 69–70, 73
laziness, 31
Lewis, Carl, 125
Lincoln, Abraham, 102
lists, to-do, 133–5
Locke, Edwin, 114
London Business School, 235
long hours, 241, 246–8

M25, 55–6
McGrath, Joseph, 121
managers
   and conflicting time preferences, 43
   disciplined time, 54
meals, rushing, 62
meandering person, 166, 168
meaning
   combining with challenge, 96
   combining with pleasure, 98
   as source of happiness, 91–2, 97–8,
     99, 100, 101
medicine, taking, 68
meetings, 207–20
   agenda, 211–12
   changing time cultures, 243–6
   facets of successful time generator,
     207–8
   getting support, 213–14
   guest list, 210
   keeping on track, 215–16
   location, 210–11
   setting the stage, 209–14
   and spontaneous people/planners,
     35
   stimulating participation, 216–17
   taking out the tension, 217–19
   talking at, 211–12
   without chairs, 213
mental and direction-setting exercise,
   106
Mind Gym Online, 8–9, 259
mindlessness, 254
mirrors in lifts, 46
mission, writing a personal, 100–1
monochrons, 39
morning people see Larks
motivation ways of increasing, 119–20

multi-tasking, 39
'my time isn't my own', 49–52

needy person, 166, 169–71
night, biological, 69
no, saying, 149, 172–81

off loading see delegation
overcommitment, 139–49
   and burnout, 148–9
   curing, 139–45
   prevention, 145–8
Owls, 70, 73

PACE process, 160–2
parasites see time parasites
Pareto principle, 26, 144
Parkinson's Law, 121, 248
pathfinder, 103–13
Pavlov, 234
perfection, belief in, 80
Pershing, D. Lynne, 53
persistent offenders, 165–71
personal recommendations, 233
pest control programme, 10, 13
physical and direction-setting exercise,
   105
pie-chart and direction-setting exercise,
   110–12
places happiest in the world, 90
planners, 33, 34, 35–6, 43, 44–5
   quick fixes for harassed, 40
planning fallacy, 124–5
planning (for non-planners), 123–36
   advantages and disadvantages,
     123–4
   impact on business performance,
     123–4
   'padding' out plans, 135
   scenario, 135
   and to-do lists, 133–5
   and visualisation, 125–30, 131–2
   writing plan up, 130–1
pleasure, 99, 101
   combining with challenge, 95
   combining with meaning, 98
   as source of happiness, 90, 93–5, 99,
     101
pointers using of in speed reading, 188,
   193, 199
politicians evading questions, 179–80
polychronic people, 39
Positive Psychologists, 90
precision delegation, 222–4, 226, 227,
   229
preferences, time see time preferences
present, concentrating on, 65–6, 120

presentation skills, 118
procrastination, 77–86, 124
    common beliefs leading to, 80–3
    quick fixes to changing our beliefs, 84–6
    rethinking unhelpful beliefs, 83–4
'psychological contracts', 229
psychological games, 146–7
public speaking and goal getting, 118–19
punctuality, 32
purpose, 2
pushy person, 166, 169

quality
    equals time myth, 53–4
    and saying no, 174
questionnaires
    are you burnt out?, 149
    are you a rushaholic?, 57–9
    design you own programme, 15
    finding your time preference, 36–7
    how you consider time, 24–5, 28–9
    and interruptions, 158–60
quiet time, 247

rapture, 95
Razran, Gregory, 234
reading fast see speed reading
Redgrave, Steve, 125
Reinhardt, Luke The Diceman, 103
relational contracts, 229
relationships
    and direction-setting exercise, 108
    and mismatched time preferences, 42
relativity, 52
reputation and saying no, 173–4
right environment, belief in, 82
Rosenman, Ray, 60
Rotter, Julian, 50
rushaholics, 55–66
    and alarm call, 63–4
    and decision-making, 61
    estimating how long something will take, 64
    judging, 61–2
    living life in future, 65–6
    questionnaire, 57–9
    reducing of pleasure, 62–3
    techniques to find a calmer way, 61–6

scanning, 202
scenario planning, 135
second wind, 164
self-control and saying no, 173
self-employed, 2

self-esteem, 26
    and saying no, 173
Seligman, Martin, 90
Seneca, 1, 258
shift work, 74
skimming, 202
'sleep camels', 74
sleep deprivation, 74
Slow Food Movement, 62
Snow, Sophia, 47
social direction-setting exercise, 106
speed reading, 62, 182–204
    bad habits, 187–8
    and fixations, 193–4, 199
    reading without reading, 200–2
    removing subvocalisation, 187, 188, 199
    and scanning, 202
    and skimming, 202
    Test (1), 183–7
    Test (2), 188–93
    Test (3), 194–8
    trouble shooting, 198–9
    using pointers, 188, 193, 199
speeding up see rushaholics
spontaneous people, 33, 34–6, 37–8, 43, 44–5
    quick fixes for disorganised, 40–1
stretch goals, 117–20, 122
subvocalisation, 187, 188, 199
supermarket visits, 99–100
Superslow movement, 56
swimmers, 68

talking to oneself see subvocalisation
teams
    matching concentration curves, 74–5
    and time preferences, 43
Thatcher, Margaret, 179–80
thinking mode, 254, 255
time cultures, 239–49
    changing, 242–8
    destructive, 241–2
    getting on with own work, 246–8
    and meetings, 243–5
    and working parties, 245–6
Time Doves see Doves
time generators, 251–2, 255–8
Time Hawks see Hawks
time parasites, 251–2, 255, 255–8
time poor people getting time with, 230–8
time preferences, 32–45
    borrowing behaviours from other, 38–41
    coping with other people's, 42
    planned, 33, 34, 35–6, 40, 43, 44–5

questionnaire, 36–7
spontaneous, 33, 34–6, 37–8, 40–1,
    43, 44–5
and teams, 43
time on your own, 148
to-do lists, 133–5
toxic time cultures *see* time cultures
transactional contracts, 229

unconscious beliefs *see* beliefs,
    unconscious
underestimating, 124–5
unreliable person, 165, 167

veterans, war, 99
visualisation and planning, 125–30,
    131–2

waiting rooms, 152, 155
waiting for someone, 152–3, 155
washing up, 48
wealth and happiness, 89
work, 97–8
    balance with life, 48
    direction-setting exercise, 107
    and flow, 117
    label of, 47–9
working parties, 245–6
worrying, 163

Xerox, 66

Without whom

'The Mind Gym: give me time' was written by Octavius Black and Sebastian Bailey, co-founders of The Mind Gym. However, it would never have happened without the counsel, enterprise and remarkable commitment of many others.

The academic board chaired by the illustrious Professor Guy Claxton* and including Professor Michael West*, Professor Ingrid Lunt*† and Emeritus Professor Peter Robinson*.

The Mind Gym core team past and present, led during writing purdah by the indomitable Sam Aspinall, and including Sam Scott, Deborah Taylor, Pui-Wai Yuen, Ben Oxnam, Joe McLewin, Caroline Smith, Rebecca McGuire-Snieckus, Garry Scott, Jonna Sercombe, Sean Clemmit, Jonathan Law, Rachel Newton, Georgie Selleck, Joanna Yates, Tania Stewart, Nicole Evans, Daz Aldridge, Norman Lo, Pui-Kei Chan, Azim Khan, Camilla West, Sarah Pearce, Cezzaine Haigh, Alice Jackson, Elizabeth Vivian-Wright, Laura Herrod, Jessica Taylor, Tamzyn Scott, Megan Korsman.

The pioneers who continue to embrace The Mind Gym and bring it into their organisations, not just occasionally but as a cornerstone for the development of their people and growth of their business. In particular, David Murphy, Sarah Bailey and Mandy Hossami (BT); Peter Wilkinson (Royal Mail); Emma Pace, Bjorn Blanchard and Kate Spur (CSFB); Caroline Dove, Louise Kordel and Christian Hobson (Merrill Lynch); Claire Walton, Craig Sclare and Rachel Helson (Dixons); Jenny Morris and Jade Starrett (Diageo); Ian Williams and Carol Houghton (Fujitsu); Stuart Rose, Keith Cameron, Sue Round and Paula West (Marks & Spencer); Noel Hadden (Deutsche Bank); Chris Peck (GSK); David Lavarack and Laura Evans (Barclays); Peter Hallard (BBC); Hannah Betts (HBOS); Deborah Morley (Cardiff Council); Lisa Day and Margaret Bruinsma (Pfizer); Kate Purkis (ITV); Louise Cole (Royal College of Nursing); Jennifer Wight (Healthcare Commission); Stephen Webb (Transport for London); Franklin Vrede (ABN-Amro); Shailesh Patel (EDF); Maggie Hurt (National Grid).

Coaches who have delivered workouts in 360 organisations and 27 countries. In particular, John Nicholson, Simon Rollings, Samantha De Siena, Catherine Nicholson, Danny Easton, Karen Sigalas, Andrew Pearson, Steph Oerton, Jane Palmer, Jenny Flintoft, Sandra Chewins, Tony Brook, Andrew Mallett, Deborah Brown, Susan Mulholland, Clare Amos, Jessica Chivers, Catherine Semark, Jacqueline Farrington, Reuben Milne, David Ruef, Shona Garner, Paul Schrijnen, Mary Gregory, Helen Vandenberghe, Caspar Berry, Annie Ingram, Claire Castell, Patrick Medd, Sam Paulette, Tom Blaisse, Tracy Gunn, Laurie Carrick, Scott Keyser, Becky Heino, Gina Caceci, Justin Wise, Barbara Henders, Philip Woodford, Ben Avery, Nicky Moran, Fiona Houslip, Barbara Rock, Fernando Caramazana, Jane Ferguson, Nick Hastings, Frank O'Halloran, Mark Gawlinski, Wolfgang Erharter, David Stevenson, José Maria Ruperez, Jolyon Hammond, Teresa Lawlor, Andy Collett, Kate Sirrell, Charlie Curtis, Michael Lesker, John Ford, Dan Unkefer, Robyn Stratton-Berkessel.

The team who came together to build The Mind Gym Online: Nick Taylor, Dom Pardoe, Nigel Colvert, Richard Gough.

Those who commented on or in other ways helped the evolution from first draft to what you have in your hands: Professor Adrian Furnham, Ben Cannon, John Smythe, Brinsley Black, David and Rosemary Gordon-Steward, Natalie Hourihan, Liz Dore, Janie van Hool.

Editors and journalists who featured 'The Mind Gym: wake your mind up': Cath Ostler, Tiffanie Darke, John-Paul Flintoff, Rebecca Alexander, Clare Longrigg, Emilie McMeekan, Mathew Gwyther, Emma De Vita, Dave Waller, Claire McDonald, Annabel Cutler, Elizabeth Cocozza, Bill Turnbull, Simon Mayo, Vanessa Gilmour, Camilla Long, Deirdre Sanders, Melissa Porter, Helen Kirwan-Taylor, Danuta Kean and, in Ireland, Pat Kelly, Kate Holmquist, Lisa Jewell, Marianne Hanifin, Paula Shields, Annette O'Meara.

Lucinda Gordon Lennox for her unswerving support despite the pressure of her banking exams.

Juliet Bailey for her forbearance and understanding when the writing coincided with the birth of Genevieve.

Tif Loehnis of Janklow Nesbit, without whom none of The Mind Gym books would ever have existed, and Jo Dickinson whose exceptional judgement and sensitive advice makes her an editor any author would relish.

Mandy Wheeler, Managing Director of Punch it up, for her unequivocal advice, unstinting dedication, extensive psychology knowledge and deft way with words.

The greatest thanks of all are due to the tens of thousands of people who take part in workouts and share, every day, what they do and don't like. These honest (sometimes very honest) views are the basis on which The Mind Gym is constantly revised, refreshed and renewed. We hope that, as a reader of this book, you too will share your opinions and so make sure that The Mind Gym constantly improves and consistently gives you what you want. Well, as near as.

(*= Fellow of the British Psychological Society; † = former President of the British Psychological Society)

Will you make the most of what's inside?

In much of our lives, our minds operate on autopilot. Rather like the tourist who repeats the same words louder each time the local doesn't understand, we tend to continue thinking and behaving in similar ways, even if this isn't getting us what we want.

However, once we can spot these mental habits, we can change them.

As a result, we are more likely to

- achieve more in less time
- gain energy and have less negative stress
- resolve difficult challenges
- win people round to our point of view
- enjoy life

Over 100,000 people have taken part in and recommended The Mind Gym's workouts. Now, for the first time, hundreds of these practical tips and techniques based on applied psychology are packed into *'The Mind Gym: **wake your mind up'*** and, with your free personal membership number, at The Mind Gym Online.

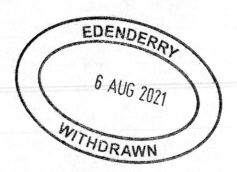